Follow The Forage For

BETTER BASS ANGLING

Volume 2 - Techniques

by Larry Larsen

Book II in the Bass Series Library

A LARSEN'S OUTDOOR PUBLISHING BOOK
THE ROWMAN & LITTLEFIELD PUBLISHING GROUP, INC.
Lanham • Chicago • New York • Toronto • Plymouth, UK

Published by
LARSEN'S OUTDOOR PUBLISHING
An imprint of The Rowman & Littlefield Publishing Group, Inc.
4501 Forbes Boulevard, Suite 200, Lanham, Maryland 20706
http://www.rlpgtrade.com

Estover Road, Plymouth PL6 7PY, United Kingdom

Distributed by National Book Network

British Library Cataloguing in Publication Information Available

Library of Congress Cataloging-in-Publication Data Available

Library of Congress 88-92906   Volume 2

ISBN: 978-0-936513-04-1 (paper : alk.paper)

☉™ The paper used in this publication meets the minimum
requirements of American National Standard for Information
Sciences—Permanence of Paper for Printed Library Materials,
ANSI/NISO Z39.48-1992.

Printed in the United States of America

CONTENTS

SECTION III. Feeding Bass Catchers

1 **Pattern Development**   151
    Beneath The Waves And Beyond

2 **The Action Imitators**   169
    Lures That Move Like The Forage

3 **The Natural Finishes**   183
    Resemblance Of Plugs To Bass Forage

4 **Worming Theories**   193
    From The Kinky To The Natural

5 **King of Live Baits**   207
    Shine For Lunker Bass

SECTION IV. Better Bass Angling Strategies

6 **Aquatic Vegetation**   227
    The Right Cover For Food

7 **Feeding Bass**   245
    Schoolers Are More Catchable

8 **Nocturnal News**   255
    The Active Time Of Forage

9 **Wood Habitats**   271
    Where Baitfish Congregate

III.
FEEDING BASS
CATCHERS

Pattern Development
Beneath The Waves And Beyond

MOST ANGLERS AGREE that locating bass is the difficult part of filling a stringer. Many fishermen can put bass in the boat if you 'put them on fish', but the real separation between the consistent bassmen and the occasional catchers of fish is in the consistent finding. Once fish are located, then technique and tackle become paramount in establishing a pattern, as well as staying with the fish. The most successful bassmen in this country are well aware of the concept of "pattern fishing" They apply it to natural lakes and rivers, as well as to huge manmade reservoirs.

Many anglers think in terms of relating lure parameters, such as size, color and action, and fishing technique, to the existing conditions of habitat, weather, and forage, but . . . few are really successful. To make "patterning" work, one has to continually think. As conditions change, so must lures and technique, and often, trying several things is required before a productive pattern can be established.

Most tournament professionals strive to establish four or five different fish producing patterns during the contest's practice period. This way, hopefully, one or two will remain consistent producers during the days of competition.

While the tournament professionals may like to have four or five different fish-producing patterns established during a contest's practice period, they'll hope that one or two of these will remain a consistent producer during the days of the tournament. If a pattern can be established early in the day, most weekend fishermen can end up with a good catch.

If a pattern can be established early in the day, most weekend anglers can end up with a good catch. The key, of course, in establishing what a successful pattern might be on a particular day, is to try several types of lures in several different types of water. Once a couple of bass are caught, some assumptions can be made and possibly a good pattern isolated, which may produce elsewhere on the same body of water.

Most anglers have specific locations and conditions under which they prefer to fish, but tournament pros do not spend a great deal of time on one type of cover unless it is hot. Time wasted on an unproductive area could be time well spent searching other types of cover and structure.

Likewise, an angler who throws a crank bait all day long, with little or no success, is less apt to find a good pattern than one whose versatility allows him to toss worms, spinnerbaits, and top water plugs. The most successful anglers establish a good productive pattern early and stay with it until it fades. They work hard to establish it and are constantly changing lures and locations until they find producers.

Several years ago, I was fishing a major bass tournament circuit's final championship, as a press observer. I had two great partners who were able to put together effective patterns and to place highly in the final event. Both weighed in limits during the tourney.

I fished the final day with Charlie Foster of Kings Mountain, North Carolina. He had discovered a worm-bullrush pattern plus a second, more productive pattern. Charlie had found a good drop-off in a canal down river (St. Johns) from Florida's Lake Monroe, which held a lot of small bass of just keeper size. Suspicions rose as to whether any patterns would hold for the third day, after the cold front had moved through in round two. The tournament start was delayed two and one-half hours on that final day due to the 25 mile per hour winds and 40 degree temperatures.

Charlie headed to his 'number one pattern' hole and anchored. I watched as he tossed Texas-rigged worms and a small crank bait. His first bass, a 'short', came aboard about 15 minutes after our arrival and another small ten incher tried to escape with Charlie's worm about 20 minutes later, but the larger, keeper size weren't present.

Backup Pattern

Charlie made the decision then, to take a 15 minute run back up the river to try his bullrush pattern along the somewhat wind protected lake shoreline. It was a good move. We motored into the cove where he and Junior Samples (of Hee-Haw fame) had taken two nice sized bass apiece the previous day.

"We should be able to catch larger fish in here if they're still around," Charlie said. "Junior had one on in here over ten pounds that got off yesterday," he added. Being an observer, I couldn't say anything or give the contestant any information that might help him unfairly, over another, but I had caught my largest fish the day before in that general area.

We were able to work the boat close to the bullrushes in the cove and evade the wind a little. The first 100 yards was unproductive and we were beginning to wonder whether the front had pushed the bass from the three feet of water. I noticed fish movement in the rushes and had confidence we would catch some shortly...unless my partner wanted to move.

Luckily, he had a strike and although he missed the fish, his confidence in the area remained. Charlie moved the boat fairly fast with the trolling motor until fish were found. This actually left me a few shots at places he hadn't cast to. It was into one of these places that I threw a crank bait behind the boat, into a bullrush pocket.

I retrieved it about three feet before a fat two pounder pounced on it. I flipped it into the live well as Charlie turned the boat to come back toward the area. My second cast resulted in another bass of about one and one-half pounds on the same Balsa-B bait. I laid my rod down and said, "They're all yours."

I then watched Charlie take four bass, lose two good ones, and miss several strikes from the same ten foot by ten foot pocket in the rushes. I took pictures, ate, changed lures, and messed around for about three hours, while Charlie tossed crank baits and worms into the 'hole' (three feet deep) from our anchored position.

Finally, the action slowed and Charlie upped anchor and started to move away from the pocket back into the small cove. "You through with the hole?" I asked.

"Yea, go ahead and cast in there," he replied. So, I let loose a long, lofty cast over the motor which hit at the far edge of the pocket against the bullrushes. The long, black worm had just reached the bottom when my arms were almost jerked out of their sockets by the strike.

I set back hard on the bass and after a good fight, which included three jumps for a nearby camera boat, the six pound, nine ounce largemouth was netted by Charlie. You never saw a boat turn around and re-anchor as fast as Charlie's did then.

Why had the fish held in that shallow water after the cold front came through? The snail beds that covered the bottom in that particular area, kept the concentration of bass there. My crank bait continuously hooked snails as it bumped the bottom on the retrieve.

Everything worked out for both of us, as my bass was the tournament's Big Bass and won me a trip to Lake Guerrero, and Charlie held on to his second place spot to finish $3,200.00 richer.

Natural Waters

Lake Arietta is a dishpan body of water near Auburndale, Florida. It is typical of many natural ponds and lakes, with its shallow perimeter of grass and rushes, gradually sloping shorelines, and light samples of scattered hydrilla and coontail along the bottom.

Waters "chock-full" of heavy cover are hard to pattern with a sinking lure or semiweedless-type lure. It has to be very weedless! This is the type of area though that most fishermen pass over, and you can have a ball catching a string of bass from the jungle within.

Polk County guide, Bob Lowe and I spent our mid-afternoon there on a hot, early May day. The wind was calm, the lake's surface glassy, and of course, fish movement (feeding) was not apparent. The conditions were tough, and the only way we could expect some bass was through quickly patterning them.

Bob was very familiar with Arietta and quickly eliminated the potential grass and bullrush shallow water pattern. The clear, calm water and mid-day sun dictated other, more feasible patterns.

We started tossing purple worms in the 8 to 12 feet depths about 30 yards from shore and we soon established a productive pattern. The largemouth were holding in clumps of hydrilla and gobbled up our plastic worms when they were retrieved over the mini-structure. Experimentation proved sinker weight to be critical in teasing a strike. One-eighth ounce bullet-shaped worm weights were ideal; one-quarter ounce was simply too heavy and sank deeply into the patches of submerged aquatic plants.

We searched the productive depths of the hydrilla that was not apparent from the surface. The clumps were usually 20 feet across, so once our lures bumped into the aquatic structure, we could toss out in the same direction a second or third time with a good chance of again contacting the hydrilla and nearby bass.

From Bob's initial cast, which resulted in a two pound bass, activity continued for the following hour and one-half, just as long as our weighted wigglers crawled across a hydrilla clump. We found five or six such clumps, each giving up a couple of largemouth, but the size was not impressive. Most of the bass ranged between one and two pounds and a lunker was not to be had.

We finished out that day's short trip looking over the lake and checking our other patterns (which were unproductive). The only working pattern that we were able to establish on Arietta would have, I'm sure held for the remainder of the day, but other commitments ended that short trip.

Changing Patterns

Patterning bass one day doesn't necessarily mean the following day will repeat. Again, the circumstances dictate patterns. On another occasion, small schools of bass were breaking the surface periodically, all round us. It was the summer 'season' for schoolers; August, and the 90-plus degree days seemed conducive to the late afternoon antics of the yearling bass.

The activity centered around a one hour time-slot just prior to sundown and darkness. Mostly in the one pound class, the schoolers did have a few surprises in the form of an occasional 'thick shouldered' three pounder. The schools of bass moved along underneath roving masses of shad and 'cut' into them, seemingly without provocation.

My two fishing partners that day began angling for the late afternoon surface feeders with Texas-rigged worms, while I chose a Bagley crank bait, the Small Fry Shad. The medium running plug has a unique silver foil finish which, I feel, adds to the visibility of such a lure and, correspondingly, to its productivity.

The bass were foraging on small, two-inch shad and the shad-shaped lure certainly did its job. I caught and released two dozen bass in the hour of fishing, as my partners managed less than 10 between them on their worm rigs. One of them did switch to a gold-finish crank bait during that period, but it produced little.

The silver foil-finish bait more closely resembled the coloring of the forage (than did the gold) and had a smaller diving lip, making it a shallower running lure. The schools of baitfish were at, or immediately under the lake's surface and the shallow-running shad bait moved through the same depths. Thus, it outproduced the others.

The following evening found us sitting in the same spot, searching for the breaking fish. The activity on top had slowed and the high winds appeared to have a definite effect. The schools of bass were surfacing randomly in a much wider area than on the previous night, and a slightly different pattern was discovered.

The conditions, I felt, called for small shad-type lures that could be cast long distances to the visible surface feeders. I chose a Little George tail spinner to meet these requirements and tossed it at any swirl within the proverbial 'country mile'. It was very productive, considering the sparce groups of breaking fish.

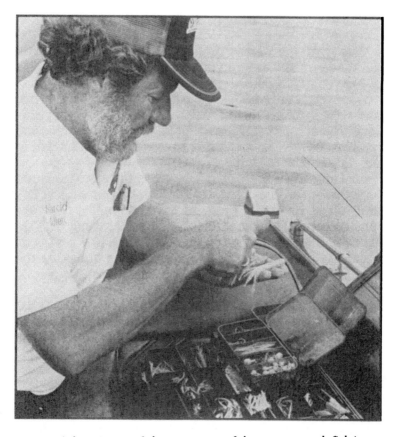

*Pattern fishing is one of the most successful means to catch fish in to-
day's world. The most productive anglers establish a good productive
pattern early and stay with it until it fades. They work hard to establish
it and are constantly trying different types of lures in a variety of areas
until they find the pattern.*

My partners experimented with several baits but stuck
mainly to plastic worms. Their worms took a toll on the
bottom-hugging schools in the area. They each caught and
released over twenty largemouth which matched my production on the George.

Forage Movement

Why were the worms productive the second night and not the first? The conditions were different and the schools of bass were structured differently.

Wind tends to break up the schools of small forage fish and actually blows them around. High winds and roily surface waters make it difficult for the angler to see topside activity, as well as making it harder for predator fish to see, follow, and grab their favorite morsel, the shad.

Concentrations of feeding bass schools are generally not as prevalent as in calmer weather, but the numbers of fish are still in the same area. In the high winds, they are 'unstructured', to some extent, and not cruising in huge schools, beneath the shad schools. They are scattered about the area randomly and are prone to attacking the deadliest lure for bass under such conditions, the plastic worm.

My lure, the George, produced as many largemouth as the worm, but the fish were up and down so fast that I had to hit right on top of the surface activity within 5 seconds, or simply forget it. Tossing to sparse, widely ranging schools can often be slow under these conditions. Still, it provided near-surface activity that the other plugs in my tackle box weren't up to for that occasion.

The fish were patterned, but the pattern was changing. Fortunately, many of the parameters were the same from one evening to the next, resulting in only minor alterations to the previous day's productive pattern.

Pattern Check Out

Most forage-intensive waters are, by nature, weedy and generally have some sort of a weedline. The weedline points should generally be worked prior to checking out other portions of the weeds. After that, the angler should forget working the entire weedline and just look at the shore. Many times the shoreline can give a good indication

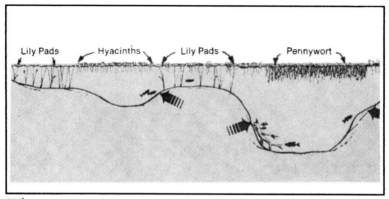

When a variety of aquatic plants are present in an area of the lake or river, knowing the bottom conditions that each species thrives in or over can be a big help. In this case, the long-rooted pennywort with its intertwined root system is found over deeper water. Pads growing a distance from shore reveal the presence of shallower and softer bottom. Hyacinths will hold over open water but not to the extent that pennywort will.

of the best area to search for productive patterns, while the weeds in the lake may all look alike. For example, the bass will normally be back in the weeds in the spring, inside this weedline. After spawning, they often move to the weedline nearest a drop-off to set up home for the summer.

The entire weedline should be checked for a drop-off. Weedlines don't just happen! There has to be a reason for the weeds to end and not propagate beyond a certain point. It is normally because the depth limits the light penetration, and this is usually what our quarry seeks! Once a weedline pattern is discovered, it may hold and be productive for several days, as long as similar conditions prevail.

Anglers looking for the best pattern can make a big mistake by assuming that shallow waters have only flat bottoms. Many bass fishermen think along the same lines, and that's why there are still many large bass available to be caught. Natural lake bottoms abound with sink holes, rock out-croppings, springs, fallen trees and creek beds. All of this can be in shallow water and 'patternable'.

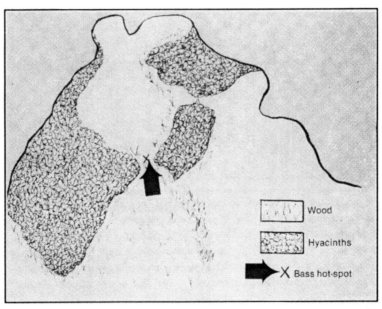

The combination of the flooded trees and the floating water hyacinths which are "stacked up" act as a funnel to concentrate forage and bass. Watch for these bottlenecks or funnels at all times. Many things can create them such as floating or submerged vegetation, wooded areas or even shallow close-together flats with deeper water running between them.

Since good habitat provides food and comfort to a bass, understanding how to recognize this structure is important in establishing a productive pattern. It is often hard to concentrate on finding patterns when the eye is full of beautiful cypress trees loaded with Spanish moss flitting in the breeze, with a field of pads growing between the trees and the boat. Spanish Moss has an aesthetic value when combined with picturesque cypress or old oak, and the fishing cast's drawing-power is tremendous.

Probably the most important thing a pattern fisherman can do is learn to read the shallow water areas. Many keys to bottom structure exist at the surface for the careful observer.

Underwater Spy

To think though, that fish always prefer to be in shallow water, is wrong. Their safety and protection lies 180 degrees from ours. The fish retreats to deep water and spends most of his time there, just as we spend the majority of our time on dry land (where we feel most comfortable).

The primary period when bass spend any length of time in the shallows, is when they are spawning, and this is a biological urge. I had an interesting dive in a small lake near my home one February during the spawning period. Several male bass had fanned debris away from their nests which were all constructed in three feet of water, near the edge of a drop-off.

The lake was man-made and dug for the purpose of getting fill for an interstate highway which passed nearby. The banks were deep due to a scoop that made a straight cut along them, which is probably why most of the spawning bass that I saw, were around an island. The island's shallow shores and heavy cattails provided the bass with excellent cover.

The island had a shallow 3 foot deep 'flat' that fell into a sheer drop-off running down to 15 feet. The exceptionally clear lake had a visibility of 10 to 15 feet and had heavy vegetation growth in most of the shallows.

The beds were all located in the light, outside stalks about five feet from the drop-off. I descended to about seven feet and moved along in the deeper water, keeping the shallows at eye-level in front of me. The first bed I noticed, had a young male bass of about one pound on it. As I approached slowly, he moved off and retreated four feet to the rear, toward the island.

When I neared the bed, he moved forward slightly, keeping me straight in front of him. He just hovered there, keeping an eye on me. I stuck out my hand over the bed and wiggled my finger. He then started forward again, stopping two feet away from the bed and my hand.

Prolific growths of vegetation such as pepper grass, lily pads, sawgrass, cattails, and maiden cane is one place to begin your search for spring patterns. Look for small baitfish, schools of small fish and swirls of larger bass. The alert fisherman who spots movement in the weeds or vegetation and knows what to do about it will bring in the biggest bass. The male bass will often build the nest in holes or openings.

"Pugnacious" was an appropriate description of him.

I did see three large females of five to eight pounds in the very heavy cattails behind the beds. I believe that their roe was probably ripe and they were near dropping. Each of them took off for the deep water as I neared their area. For me, it was a very interesting and informative dive. This explained something about bass behavior during their spawning activities, but I would certainly not expect similar responses during the summer, fall, and winter. I'm sure that they would move then, to the deep water structure in that lake.

Shallow Pattern

Bass will not be in deep water, however, if the structure is not present. On another lake, a friend and I explored the depths with SCUBA, searching for bass haunts. The lake was also man-made and averaged about six feet in depth. This mid-summer dive proved to me that cover (or structure) is more important than deep water alone. We scouted the entire lake and a canal which was dug to a constant 20 feet. The only game fish present, with one exception were in heavy cattails and weeds near the shore, but next to a deep water drop-off. The lake was very clear, but a layer of silt covered most of the bottom.

We cruised the 20-foot deep canal and six-foot deep lake near the bottom and saw nothing! It was a barren wasteland with no cover. As we swam along, we would, from time to time, kick up the silt which would cloud up the immediate area.

The fish that we discovered in the dense cover headed for protection in a predictable, but interesting fashion. The bluegill and small sunfish swam back into heavier cover in slightly shallower water, presumably since their most common enemy is larger fish. They were hesitant about going into barren, deep water where they could not hide behind anything.

The large bass, on the other hand, shot out of the weeds upon spotting us and disappeared into the depths. Since their predators are many times animals or air-breathing creatures of larger proportions, they felt a retreat to the deep water environment would shake loose whatever it was that was approaching.

Feeding Smarts

Lunker bass have a "smart" territory in a body of water receiving normal fishing pressure. They are able to forage and grow to impressive sizes because they are totally in-tune with their immediate surroundings - the habitat, the forage, and their predators.

"Big fish are more aggressive feeders than the smaller ones and they forage more often," says Doug Hannon. "That's why anglers on a virgin lake will normally catch, or at least have on, the big bass first." For the same reason, the Bass Professor notes, lunker bass cannot be transplanted into heavily fished waters. The highly aggressive feeders will not be in the "smart" territory which they have developed over several years, and they will soon be caught, regardless of any pattern being established.

Doug's tagging studies and experimentation have shown this to be true. Over the last several years, he has tried to influence the supply of big fish available in a particular lake by catching some from another and moving them to the new territory. His experiments had two purposes: one -verification that a lake with heavy pressure on lunker bass could have that supply replenished immediately, and two -determination of the possibility of developing a trophy class fishery in a particular body of water.

"Several big fish were caught, tagged, and released in a different lake. These particular bass lasted less than a week or two normally, before their aggressive feeding caused capture," he says. The results were attained from calls received from the lucky anglers. Doug's tags are imprinted with a fish I.D. number and the telephone number where he can be reached. His records have each tagged fish logged in with pertinent data on length, girth, approximate weight, etc. Being able to pattern a bass in its "smart" territory is the ultimate achievement.

Fun Pattern

The hot, June sun was beginning to bead sweat on our foreheads as we started to plug for any sized bass with our lightweight lures. We worked the baby baits in and around brush in five feet of water and took two quick bass limits. How we hit upon the pattern rates as a very memorable experience for me.

"I'm going to have some fun," Guy said, as he laid down the Texas-rigged worm outfit with 25 pound test line and picked up an ultralight outfit with his 'fun' lure, a floating-minnow imitation attached to 14 pound test line.

A frequent fishing partner, Guy Settlemeyer and I had been searching three hours for largemouth, preferably lunker-size, with very little success. A couple of small two pound bass were the result of our 'hawg-hunting'.

Guy's second cast with the plug to some small, submerged trees was retrieved three feet before the lure stopped and Guy set back hard on the fish. The huge bass leaped a foot clear of the lake's surface, throwing water everywhere. I didn't have time to think about how impressive it was for the gigantic bass to clear the surface on a jump. I dropped my rod and grabbed the net.

Guy strained at the rod working the fish free of a submerged tree trunk that it had tried to swim around. The lunker again leaped, clearing the surface and headed for deeper, open water, much to Guy's (and my) relief.

Guy worked the fish closer to the boat and the lunker's final leap showed some signs of her tiring. I'm sure my partner was also showing signs of tiring, but I couldn't take my eyes off the bass as I readied the net to end the battle.

The ultralight rod was bent double as Guy exerted the pressure required to force her ascent toward the surface. As the lunker's head came into view from the tannic-acid stained waters, I quickly slid the net in front of her and scooped up the monster. The small plug still had a firm grasp on it's predator's lower jaw, but who knows how long the line might have held. Guy was glad to have her aboard.

Guy Settlemeyer with his 15 pound, ½ ounce 'package of fun' which established a productive pattern to save our trip that day.

The bass was truly a monster; her sides were thick and powerful and she was the most healthy and fit 'hawg' that I had ever seen. This fish made the twelve pounder that I had caught on the previous trip seem like a baby, and it did so without displaying a fat gut, which is typical of many lunkers over ten pounds.

The fish caught on Guy's light outfit and 'fun' lure was weighed six hours later on state-inspected scales and registered in at 15 pounds and one-half ounce. Not a bad package of fun for anyone, it was the largest bass that Guy had ever caught.

BETTER BASS ANGLING

THE ACTION IMITATORS
Lures That Move Like The Forage

L URE TECHNOLOGY TODAY is more advanced than ever in terms of both shape and coloration. Competing against all those living creatures which make up the forage base in the bass' environment is tough. The lure that most closely resembles the action and appearance of the real prey will generally be the most productive.

Effective lures require a natural forage look and the appropriate action. One without the other is usually a worthless producer, except on younger bass. The angler tossing the right lure will catch the lunker.

Several factors enter into the degree of importance placed on lure action: water clarity, cover density, and depth. Bass experience variations of all factors and their senses are atuned to the environment.

In clear water, lure action and resemblance are equally vital to the bait's success. Bass rely heavily on their sight to select and capture forage. Lure speed under such conditions should be rapid, since time-lapse is increasingly detrimental when fishing a counterfeit bait. When water clarity changes to dingy after a heavy rain, sight-oriented fish revert to their vibration, sound detection system for feeding. Lure speed can be slowed and more emphasis should be put into copying the movement of the forage.

An advance in technology has made many lures highly effective bass-getters. Using them eliminates the problems involved in getting, keeping alive, and handling baits.

Stained-water bass have very little opportunity to examine intricate photoprint patterns on a tempting lure as it passes. These bass rely partially on their eyes, but more importantly, upon their inner ears and lateral lines to enable them to locate their forage in a seemingly 'close' environment. Lure action is vital in such areas with limited light penetration.

Water color is affected by such factors as bottom composition, run-off (drainage) fertility, rainfall, and wind. Off-color water can vary from tannic acid stained, to muddy brown, to algae-bloom green. In all types of low-clarity water, lure action is generally the predominant trigger in a bass' choice of food.

Depth of the water should be a factor in the speed of retrieve and action imparted to the lure. Slower retrieves for diving plugs are usually the rule in shallow water. Bottom-bumping worms and jigs should be slowed down in the depths for maximum structure contact. Other lures which rely on their weight for depth control should be fished similarly.

Lures relying on a diving lip are often speed-sensitive, but modifications can be made to move them deeper, to make a more vigorous side-to-side action or to make them more buoyant. Stiff rods and light lines can aid in depth control and lure action. Moving the rod tip from side to side during the retrieve can add motion to the lure. The hook can also be set more quickly with the stiff rod, when fishing a stop-and-go type plug retrieve.

Surface Weed Baits

In waters of less than five feet, surface baits are effective around the heavy weed cover. Seducing a lunker bass into coming up like thunder and murdering a bait on the surface, is an exciting feat.

While bass may be 'on the feed' at times, it will often be necessary to 'impulse' or stimulate fish into feeding when they have no inclination to do so. Attracting bass from deep in a weed bed, requires lures that can ripple the surface in a natural manner, plus a little finesse on the part of the angler. Actually, little movement is required to disturb the surface and produce audible noise. Bass in the shade and concealment of a weed bed or bonnet patch, will usually note the action above.

Not all of the favorite, heavy weed baits float. Many are used on the surface but will descend to the bottom if the line becomes slack, Since the action and control of these lures is through the rod tip, a taut line is a must.

Guiding a lure through heavy cover takes practice, and watching the line, as well as the lure, is important in preventing snags and having proper bait control. Casts should be made as short as is practical and boat movement should be minimal to prevent hangups. Casts should be made ahead of the boat as the angler works the cover fringes, so that the line of retrieve will not loop behind the boat. A more taut line means better lure control and a better hook set when needed.

Buzz Baits

In waters with heavy growth, a fast, buzzed bait is natural on the surface. A wake can oft be seen, forming behind the lure. It resembles excited forage trying to get away. Simply keep it coming fast enough to keep the spinner turning on or just under the surface and be ready to set the hook. Surface-buzzing spinner baits are among the hottest lures of any type on the market today. The lures

The buzzing-type spinner bait is deadly on near-surface fish. The blade is more effective at keeping the lure at the surface in an ultra-slow retrieve. That action and the 'squeeky' sound it makes coming across the surface are keys to the success of the lure.

generally have a blade design that pops it up on the surface and allows the fisherman to crank it back at a very slow pace, keeping the bait on top at all times.

Used around dense grass patches such as pepper grass,

sawgrass, and eel grass, the lure is normally fished with the rod tip held high. The angler should begin reeling just before the lure hits the water so that it is always on the surface. The lures are effective in both pockets and on the weed bed points. The retrieve is usually slow but can be speeded up to trigger bass into striking.

Sound is important in stained or roily waters, since visibility could be minimal. The main attractor under these conditions is the 'right' sound. In tuning the lures, generally the more used or worn the lure, the better sound quality that is produced. So, to break in this type of lure, many anglers stick them out of the window on the way to the lake and let the blade revolve a few thousand times. Harkin's Lunker Lure is the original buzz bait and probably still the most effective.

Skitter Baits

Weeds that grow to the lake's surface and then mat up and clog the water are particularly hard to fish. Many varieties of small floating plants that cover the surface, also require a special lure-type. To be an effective producer in this type of cover, it must ride easily over any heavy growth of aquatic plants.

For areas such as these, a skitter-type plug or spoon has the ability to ride the surface and hop over small obstructions. The retrieve is started just before the lure hits the water. Most of these lures ride on their backs with the hook riding up, away from the vegetation. Large bass are excited by the dancing bait and explode the surface to get a piece of the action. Whopper Stopper's Dirtybird and Bill Norman's Weed Walker are two fine lures for attracting this kind of action.

Bass will often follow these lures for 20 feet in heavy weeds, before pouncing on them. When a second wake forms behind the first (the lure's), the trick is just to keep the retrieve coming and to be ready. Once the bass has struck, keep him on the surface and coming toward the

Bass come out of weed patches in a hurry and nail your lure instantly. They have to react fast before their meal gets away, and it's hard for them to follow your lure for very long through such thick weeds. If you do see a wake forming behind your bait, let the lure fall toward the bottom, pausing your retrieve one second, and then set the hook.

To attract the bass from deep in the weed bed to the surface requires lures that can disturb the surface in a natural manner plus a little finesse by the angler. Actually, little movement is required to disturb the surface and produce some audible noise. Bass in the shade and concealment of a weed bed or bonnet patch will usually note the action above them.

boat, to prevent his diving into the heavy stuff. A trailer hook added to these offerings may increase their effectiveness.

Pad Action

A big bass is particularly hard to land from a pad jungle, but having a lure that will work well in the bonnets and provoke the strike is a major consideration. In a thick pad bed with just a few small openings of water, bass will have little time to focus on the lure and will strike instinctively at the action, sometimes even missing the lure. When they do take it solidly, some may be lost while you're trying to get them out of the entanglements.

In the really dense pad beds, the most preferable lures are fairly light so that they will scoot and crawl along on top of most pads. Being made of rubber helps their "bouncability', and the lures should also have some bulk so that they knock on pads, telegraphing mealtime to the lunkers below. This commotion and ruckus on top of the pads will drive hungry bass crazy. The bass have to rely on sound much more than sight to feed in pads. The bass needs to hear where the lure is going, since he will very seldom see it.

The lure may be on top of the pads much of the time, but to be 'awakened' by the explosion when the lure falls into the water, is not a rare occurence. Often a swirl can be noticed a few feet away from the lure as it impacts the water. The strike a few seconds later is the kind of exciting action that warrants anticipation to most bass anglers. Bill Plummer's Super Frog has a resilient body and great action for this type fishing.

Night Action

Technique is extremely important in prospecting for night prowling bass. Retrieves with the same monotonous cadence will out produce all others. Rhythm is critical at night, regardless of the lure, whether it's an Arbogast Jitterbug or a spinnerbait. The plain-vanilla, steady pulsating retrieve will be your most effective method for moonlight largemouth and smallmouth.

The bassman can cover more ground successfully if he forgets the fancy, twitch and jerk-type retrieves and learns to set the hook at the right moment. It's best to wait an instant before setting the hook on a top water lure. The angler who can resist the 'big set' upon the resounding splash, until he feels tension on the line, will net more bass. The bass that 'homes in' on the sound and then completely misses the plug will come right back if still in the vicinity.

Cold Water Action

Finding a good concentration of bass in their deep winter haunt, can be a real find, and knowing how to catch fish out of cold water is important. The successful angler positions his boat so that he can cast the lure beyond the drop-off into the shallower water. Then, when retrieved, the lure is allowed to drop off of the ledge. In wintertime, bass will hit the lure as it slowly falls, on a slack line, into the hole. The angler should be ready to strike when he notices the line twitch as a fish picks up the lure.

Texas-rigged worms, Arkie jig and eels, and spinnerbaits are excellent lures for this type of angling. The method is most effective on water of 10 or more feet in depth, and with water temperatures of 60 degrees or below. To find areas such as this, a water temperature meter and graph recorder can be beneficial.

For cold water bass fishing, the lure should always be slowed down. Since the bass are moving more slowly, so should the lure. It produces well when the bass are sluggish and a steady retrieve often allows a little more control on hook setting. Cold water usually dictates lighter line since the lure's action is less inhibited. It behaves more like a single entity acting on its own, rather than something being 'pulled' along by a greater force.

Many anglers prefer the solitude and action of cold weather bass fishing. They are particularly adept at working deep depths for large bass. Schools of large bass hold tighter in the winter months, and using the right equipment, and proper lure action will key the strikes.

Crank Action

The action leaders of the artificial lure clan are the crank baits. With these divers, it is possible to vary the depth of retrieve and action on successive casts. Normally, the reel is cranked fast for a few turns to drive the lure to an optimum depth, and then the retrieve rate is slowed to allow the crank bait to bump along the bottom. The depth of water determines the correct size and angle of diving lip. The larger and straighter the lip, the quicker the dive. Crank baits with rounded lips seem to crawl over most limbs and other structures, while those sporting long pointed ones often hangup in heavy cover or dig into the bottom. Many of the latest crank baits however, can be gently worked in and out of cover without getting involved in a permanent relationship.

Off-colored water and crank baits are made for each other, and a lure fished around heavy cover that brushes up against it, will out-produce most other baits. If it is not bumping bottom or mid-level structure, the cast may be wasted. The crank bait will often change course as it maneuvers around obstacles, and trigger a strike. The lure is 'worked through' the structure and not fast-cranked with reckless abandon.

The stop-and-go retrieve with a buoyant crank bait is deadly around heavy cover. They can be maneuvered just above hydrilla without hang-ups. Reel the lure until it hits the weeds, then pause and it'll float up. Start the pump again until it touches the weed bed. Repeat. Work the bait through holes in emergent vegetation in a similar way, or retrieve it along wooded points for great bass action. The lure resembles forage trying to find a place to hide.

Sound vibrations are extremely important to a crank bait's performance. Manufacturers have spent thousands of hours trying to "tune" their lures to the optimum frequency. The swimming action produced as the lure travels forward, dictates how the bait will vibrate. Crank bait designers look for a lure that runs 'tight' at low retrieve speeds.

Balsa lures, in particular, magnify the sound vibrations, as they move through the water medium. Plastic crank baits often have steel shot rattling in an internal body cavity to intensify their sound appeal. Which type of action a bass is looking for when feeding will vary, but the balsa wood plugs have another advantage, high floatation. The super buoyant lures are an asset in and around heavy cover. The Bagley Kill'R and Diving "B" II both have quick rising characteristics and yet are able to support heavier hooks and line than the less buoyant plugs. Their size casts a larger profile and sends out more vibration because of water displacement than slimmer models. They are deadly on bass in many situations, such as in heavy vegetation, stick-ups, and in low visibility water.

Other crank baits that produce hundreds of fish for me are Rebel's Deep Wee-R, Norman's Big "N", and Bagley's Silver Foil Shad. While the last bait is balsa, the other two are plastic lures which have built national reputations by their productiveness on bass. All three plugs have tremendous action and when coupled with a 'beautiful' body, are without peer in the crank bait world.

Crayfish Cranks

The imitation crayfish crank bait craze is upon us. These lures look and move differently than many of the forage fish plug imitations, and they should. Crayfish swim backwards when alarmed. They do so by making repeated strokes with their tail fan. The action is stop-and-go in a skipping fashion which kicks up clouds of bottom silt as they move rapidly along. A bass will normally strike such a lure during the brief pause in its zig-zag movement.

The proper retrieve to simulate the real thing should be fairly slow and erratic, and follow the bottom terrain. In shallow water, this lure should dive into every nook and cranny, as a live crayfish would when attempting to escape a predator. The flight backward should not be more than three or four feet.

Rocky bottoms are ideal for this type action retrieve. My world record Suwannee bass (line class) was caught over limestone shoals on a ¼ ounce brown Mann's Crawdad plug. Make the plug act 'scared' and impart to it short bursts of speed. In order to keep the plug down in very deep water, try adding a slip sinker. This will allow the lure to scratch along the bottom and stir up more mud.

Other Lures

Rubber worms and eels are often full of action, whether the angler imparts it or not. A full discussion of the rubber wigglers follows in a separate section. Plugs of rubber often produce a better catch than the hard baits. The Lit'l Critter by Knight Manufacturing Co., Creme Lure's Killer-Krawdad, and Mann's Cajun Crawdad all provide super action to attract crayfish-eating smallmouth and largemouth bass. The Spoiler Shad plastic imitations are also to bass what the crayfish replicas above are, good-action forage.

Top water action which resembles a bait-fish in trouble is provided by several popular lures of the floating-minnow variety. The injured forage actions of twitching and quivering often attract bass in waters shallower than eight feet. The Bang-o-lure is a great "twitcher" which has provided me numerous bass over the last decade or two. Propeller lures for choppy waters can also impart deadly action and produce many bass. The Smithwick Devil's Horse is a popular wood bait throughout the country.

Spinnerbaits are great for action-oriented bass. The blades make the vibrations and light reflections that attract the fish. I prefer a hammered blade that gives off 'flash' in a multi-directional pattern. I'll use painted blades (chartreuse is a good one) in murky water, but stick to the silver, hammered variety in clearer water.

The amount of light available affects the lure selection. If the water is extremely murky, lures with larger spinners and tandem blades should be used. This extra vibration is needed for water with restricted visibility, while a small single-bladed spinnerbait may suffice in clearer water.

There are several ways to control the depth and action of the lure. Besides the rate of reeling, other parameters include: weight of the lead head, number and length of skirts, size of worm or grub trailer, type of blade, number and size of blades, and number of beads and swivels. In general, more and larger mean slower descending.

THE NATURAL FINISHES
The Resemblance Of Plugs To Bass Forage Is More Than Coincidental

LURE ACTION IS AN important parameter in a successful attractor of bass, but in many waters, two other ingredients stand out as necessary. While muddy water bass are primarily keying-in on the action, those predators in medium to clear visibility waters want a complete package, that is, a forage shape and also natural coloration. A life-like plug that is realistic in all details will attract the bass under tough fishing conditions.

At times, bass will strike at any color scheme, but these occasions are just too rare. An imprint on a corresponding natural shape which represents a living, breathing creature is more often required under normal conditions. Under clear-water situations, the lures that most closely approximate the prevalent live forage will produce best. On the other hand, in low visibility waters the vibration will entice the bass to take a quick look at the appearance only, just prior to the strike.

The natural patterns are not going to put other, older color schemes out of business. Dark water conditions will often dictate using a plug in a contrasting color pattern that can be seen, rather than a 'camouflaged' lure. The high visibility bait with contrast (such as chartreuse) has

Water hyacinths, eel grass, and other aquatic vegetation are full of minute organisms which attract bait fish and small sport fish which, in turn, lures the predator, largemouth bass.

its place on the tackle store shelves and in tackle boxes, as do the natural lures. The two most important things that successful anglers have going for them are their brains and confidence.

While Rapala often claims the distinction of first introducing lures with a life-like appearance, credit for the invention of naturalized imprints goes to Tom Seward. Seward developed what was introduced by the Lazy Ike Company as the "Natural Ike", the first mass produced lure with a natural finish and shape. Many plug companies quickly followed suit with their own photoprint replicas.

Shape of Things

Various shapes picked up new "duds" and were transformed overnight into 'pretty' fake forage. Long, thin minnow imitations and fat, chubby baitfish counterfeits were soon on the market. Several lure manufacturers

Bass will often try for the largest prey they feel they can handle. Large shapes will trigger action under such circumstances. High and wide lure profiles that resemble members of the sunfish family can be the right stimulus.

developed a completely new shape for the adornment of beautiful forage coloration. Many have even gone so far as to carve in gill and fin features, which under some conditions (muddy water) may be meaningless to the bass. The lure's profile is, however, extremely important under both low light and bright sky conditions. I don't have to tell you how important a good silhouette projected against the sky is at night. The profile is contrasted against the only available light source. The maximum contrast with the sky, white sand bottom, etc., is the key to successful low-light angling. Bass won't see color or lure detail at night, but they will check out the form of potential food.

Bass will often try for the largest prey they feel they can handle. Large shapes will trigger action under such circumstances, high and wide lure profiles that resemble members of the sunfish family can be the right stimulus. Bass also ignore a lure too large or too small when they're feeding on a specific size of forage.

Flash Dance

Natural baitfish give off flashes when moving through the aquatic environment. Shad and foil finishes have become the top sellers for many tackle manufacturers. Lures such as Bagley's silver-foil shad give off a realistic, baitfish flash when retrieved. Pearl, silver, chrome, and white (or bone) are favorite lure colors that produce on many artificial baits.

The new transparent crank baits with metallic or foil inserts (such as Norman's Reflect'N) are extremely effective in low light conditions. At night, they reflect light from above, while in daylight, they reflect surrounding color and may even be brighter than a white-colored lure.

The shad's silver-pearl scales are difficult to copy in a lure's finish, but then we don't want iridescent plugs that are hard for the bass to see. Shad tend to blend into their primary environment, open water, but when they move into areas with cover, they stand out like 'dead' forage. Silver-sided lures are thus very productive in waters with heavy cover.

Color Considerations

Bass definitely see color, both under and above the water. Their dense medium (water) quickly filters out reds and even makes color contrast distinction at high lure speeds difficult. Bass basically see black and white as we do, and these two colors are extremely important to the predator/forage relationship.

Black reflects the least light back from its surface while white reflects the maximum amount. It will only disappear in the total absence of light. The color white is a key stimulus to bass which forage on shad and other soft-rayed baitfish. Even at night, the response from large bass may be vicious.

We've all heard about the guy who discovered several 3-inch long crappie in the stomachs of a couple of bass that he cleaned one day. He went back the following day with a white crank bait that he had added blotches to (with a black felt tip pen) and caught a quick limit of the crappie foragers. The speckled bait resembled the favorite bass forage at that time.

Red, orange, and brown are all stimulating to bass. They are the hues of the crayfish clan and are extremely visible in many stained waters. Many manufacturers produce a replica that resembles a mounted crayfish, more than a plastic or balsa wood lure. While some have lifelike claws, others omit them so that the bait appears "disarmed" to a predator.

There are various colorations to choose from when picking a crayfish fake. Matching the color (and size) of the crustacean in those waters is the key to some big bass. If unknown, stick to a dark brown, two-inch version. Variations may include colors ranging from red to green to gray. Closely match those inhabiting the water you're going to fish.

The new naturalized lures are made for areas of high forage concentrations and a productive arsenal includes several crayfish crankbaits in addition to a year's supply of worms.

Striking Triggers

"I don't see how it can hurt for a lure to be as natural as possible and to mimic," says Doug Hannon. "But, it's not going to make the lure miraculously successful," he cautions. "As a matter of fact, in some instances it could be a disadvantage because natural colors are protective measures, and these protective colorations tend to be designed to turn off predators, and not trigger those things that excite them."

The other defensive mechanism that will turn off almost any predator fish is a vertical yellow and black stripe, according to Hannon. "If they're going to be seen by the fish, they want to be perceived in a certain way and as a danger sign in nature - vertical stripes in a black and yellow pattern, like many poisonous fish, as well as wasps and bees are one of nature's danger signals."

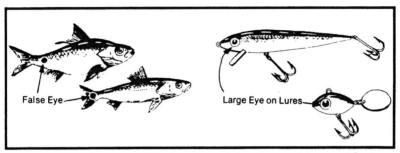

False Eye

Large Eye on Lures

Doug states, "On natural looking lures I'd rather see things emphasized that tend to trigger the predator, like an eye is a focal point for a feeding game fish to zero in on. One of the most common defense mechanisms baitfish have is their 'false eye,' which is usually toward their back end, to draw the strike away from their more vulnerable areas."

Most things that have this pattern aren't concerned about being seen. They actually depend on being seen so that they aren't confused for something that is not dangerous. By the same token, many nonpoisonous creatures mimic these colors to capitalize on their defensive characteristics. They usually are very violent and can sting or do something bad to the thing that catches them.

On natural baits, things should be emphasized that tend to trigger the fish, such as an eye. That is a focal point for a predator to strike at. One of the most common defense mechanisms on bait fish is the false eye, usually toward the tail, to draw the strike. It'll usually be much bigger than the eye on the front. It'll be a big dot and sometimes it'll be ringed in a color (such as orange) like an iris, instead of portraying just a pupil.

The predator is so distracted by the false 'eye' that he will strike the tail. Many anglers paint big eyes on their lures and they feel that they get more strikes for doing it. Fish will often follow a lure and they won't be able to find that part that they want to strike. A sense of direction is what the predator is looking for when he follows the prey and he looks for the head before he strikes. You're helping

Lures that emphasize or exaggerate the head and eye region are very productive, such as this Bagley Striper "Stick Up."

him out by putting a big eye on the lure and turning the defense mechanism of a live forage fish around. The lure is more vulnerable which excites a predator.

Lures that emphasize or exaggerate the head and eye region are very productive. The tremendous success of the "Alphabet" plugs and big balsa baits is evidence of this. Carry along a waterproof felt tip marker in the tacklebox and you're able to add or further stress the eyes on an artificial lure. A large dot in the form of a false 'eye' positioned very close to the head on each side of the lure, will serve the purpose. Separate colors for the eye (lighter shade) and pupil (darker spot) can be painted on the bait for those perfectionist anglers.

"I do think that a natural finish is not necessarily better than a lure that's chartreuse or really unnatural looking," says Hannon. "Fish can definitely see color and red is very definitely a trigger color. Red is a pretty sure color to draw an aggressive reaction. Sometimes, I paint red on the lure's head or make a bunch of red spots on it. The most benign color is green, and the fish seem to feel very secure around it. I like greens, reds, silvers, and blues the most," he says.

"Yellow is very questionable," he cautions. "It draws a strong reaction, negative or positive, and if they're hitting a yellow, fine, but yellow can be very offensive to fish. If they're not hitting a yellow lure, don't fish with it all day because it could be turning them off."

Lure Selection

Selection of the lure in most bass fishing situations is very important. Even when schools of bass are working themselves into a frenzy, feeding on surface shad and hitting about anything, more often the best strings will be taken on baits closely resembling the forage. Naturally, knowing the specie of forage should aid the angler in his choice of lures.

Most of the plugs' colors and patterns approximate the forage in the lakes and streams that you fish. The major forage species throughout the country are of the sunfish family, the crayfish, minnow species, shad (in the southern region), and perch (in the northern region). Bass see these colorations daily, and their growth is dependent upon feeding on the forage sporting those colors.

Lures imitating shad, shiners, and other soft-rayed forage are especially productive on feeding school bass. White and gray-hued lures and the popular photo-finish 'natural' color schemes seem to be bass favorites. The school bass normally chase schools of small shad, so the smaller lures are most effective.

WORMING THEORIES
From The Kinky To The Natural

WHAT IS THE MOST effective lure of all time for catching bass? Without a doubt, it has to be the plastic worm. This lure rigged in various fashions, has been accountable for reducing bass populations throughout the country, since its inception a few decades ago.

Why do worm rigs catch more than their share of predator bass? Most of the plastic wiggler rigs have one thing in common, a snake-like action. These rigs resemble the natural swimming and floating action of aquatic snakes and freshwater eels, and bass will usually hit these rigs with the intent to devour. They'll charge and smash with reckless abandon. Many times they'll leave a wake behind the rig while they catch up to it and then explode on the surface. Due to this exertion, a high percentage of fish are hooked on these rigs.

The essential ingredient in a rig is, of course, the worm. Most rigs require a super-soft, plastic worm that a fooled bass will chew on and attempt to swallow. Porous baits which are scented or 'salted' can provide additional incentive for the bass to hang on to the bait. The longer they eat the wiggler, the better the angler's chances of catching them.

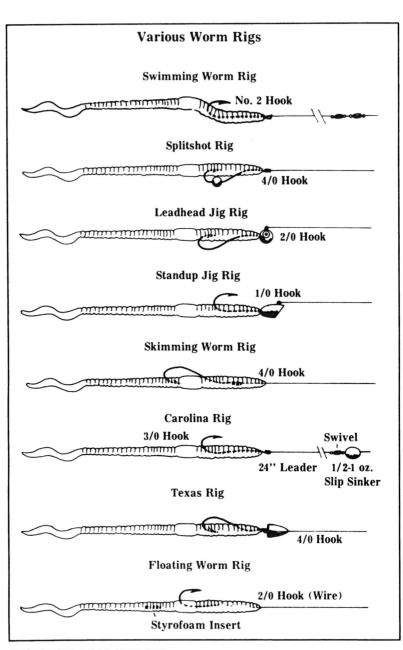

Various Worm Rigs

Swimming Worm Rig

No. 2 Hook

Splitshot Rig

4/0 Hook

Leadhead Jig Rig

2/0 Hook

Standup Jig Rig

1/0 Hook

Skimming Worm Rig

4/0 Hook

Carolina Rig

3/0 Hook

Swivel

24" Leader   1/2-1 oz.
Slip Sinker

Texas Rig

4/0 Hook

Floating Worm Rig

2/0 Hook (Wire)

Styrofoam Insert

The most popular sizes of worms range from six to eight inches. These lengths will attract keeper bass in most waters under most conditions. When getting "short" strikes, most professionals will go to a shorter length worm, such as a four-incher. This can be done by simply cutting off the front few inches, leaving a desired length. Of course, you can carry enough of the right size in the old Plano for such emergencies.

Plastic worms are built in different ways, like the aquatic creatures that they imitate. Some have legs and feet (a la salamanders) while others have thin "swimming" curled tails. Still others have long tentacles, split tails, curled arms, paddle tails, mid-body twists, hollow bodies, warts, treads, ridges and even crayfish replicas on the tail. They come in several hundred color schemes and include blood lines, metal flake glitter, flourescent, opaque, and solid options.

The Creme Scoundrel, Norman Snatrix, and Mann Augertail are some of the most popular worms for the various possible rigs. The Fishing Worm Salty Sensation, Worth Hawg Hackle, and Ditto Gatortail all have tremendous regional followings. Other worm manufacturers are producing variations that attract attention among bass chasers throughout the country.

Surface Action

The surface exploded and I turned to look at the action. My fishing partner, Steve Hamman, reared back. A chunky five-pounder hit the surface immediately, and I scampered for the landing net.

The largemouth dug for the hydrilla entanglement, but Steve's constant pressure brought her back near the surface. One more jump and I had her in the net. Steve slid the fish into my livewell next to the six-pounder I had caught earlier. Five other bass had also joined the big one before this, and the well was crowded.

"I caught that one on top, just bringing the worm across the grass," Steve commented. "Maybe they're eating

'Noisey' worming can entice hungry bass on calm or windy days in almost any kind of water.

worms on the surface now.'' Until then, we had been using Texas-rigged worms with a one-quarter ounce slip sinker. The early morning action had ceased and the old pattern was not producing.

Three casts later, Steve took another bass on the quickly-reeled, surface worm. He then took the sinker off his rig and started swimming the worm back to the boat, still at a rapid pace, and caught another four-pounder.

I quickly cut my sinker off and re-rigged. My second cast hit the water and my rapid retrieve was barely begun when the surface boiled. I lowered the rod-tip, gave the bass two seconds to chew on it, and set the hook. A three pounder was lying in our net shortly thereafter. Four casts later, Steve added a five-pounder and the action continued for another 30 minutes.

Excluding smaller bass, 16 were landed that day before the wind really began blowing and the sun came out for good. The weather had been windy and cloudy most of the day. Light rain had fallen a couple of times as a front tried to move through the area.

Skimming Worm

We were using long, nine and ten-inch plastic worms in black and purple without a weight during most of the day. I found the Creme Shimmy Granny to be my ticket. The nine-inch worm has plenty of bulk for casting without weight and a wide 'floppy' tail to wag as it skims the surface on the retrieve.

Steve termed this method the "Skimming Worm," and both of us agreed it was a success that day. We have used the rig since and it continues to be a deadly method. The long worm with self-weedless 4/0 worm hook is cast out as far as possible over hydrilla or other submerged aquatic plants, and the retrieve is started prior to its hitting the water, similar to buzzing a spinnerbait.

Most strikes will be seen, and we found a slight pause of two seconds or so to be best setting the hook. Too quick a set has usually resulted in lost fish. Seldom do bass spit out a lure they've chased so hard. If they are that actively feeding, they'll hang on.

Swimming Worm

I learned of this technique several years ago, but I didn't grasp its deadlines until a couple of space-coast bass anglers talked me into trying it. I had spent the morning on a private lake and both anglers had several bass to my couple. At lunch I re-rigged with the swimming worm at their instruction.

The rig consists of a swivel about 12 inches in front of a No. 2 straight-shanked bait hook and a threaded six-inch Creme Scoundrel worm. The swivel prevents line twists as the worm 'twirls' back to the boat on the retrieve and also adds a little weight for casting purposes.

The "only" swimming worm that works in Florida lakes, according to my teachers, is the purple Scoundrel

The Swimming Worm Rig can help turn an empty live well into a noisy one. Bass are attracted to the unique method in certain types of waters with numberous shallows.

with glo-pink tail. The body is tapered to the end of the tail on this worm, and the floppy tail of other worms would only hinder the swimming motion of the rig - that's their explanation. I've found them to be right.

I started using the rig after the sandwich break and had three fish on the first four casts. I was catching up to them as I put four more bass in the livewell in the next 30 minutes, before the wind got us again. There was a 25-mile-per-hour 'blow' that had already limited us to a small canal, which was hard to fish because its barren banks did not contain any wind-blocking cover. But I learned plenty before we quit.

The worm is threaded along the shank and the barb is brought out about one inch down the worm, so that the only thing showing is the exposed barb. The eye of the hook rests just inside the worm's head and the worm's body makes a "kink" where it follows the curve of the hook's bend.

The size of hook and the size (or number) of swivel should be judged on weight. A small, thin worm is best, and a 20-pound-test leader between the hook and swivel will keep wear and twist to a minimum in that section.

I believe the real key to the effectiveness of this rig is that the bass do not feel resistance when they take the lure. It is easier to be a line watcher with the swimmin' worm, and that's what successful worming is all about. I think many times a bass feels the slip-sinker in a conventional rig and spits it out quickly. With this rig, they'll usually grab the tail, then inhale it and chew on the whole thing. Thus, a second or two pause is best before setting the hook.

Suspended Worm

A seven or eight-inch worm has almost a neutral buoyancy with a 3/0 straight-shanked worm hook imbedded in it. If it is twitched and jerked slowly, it can be brought across or just under the surface of the water with enticing action. The worm will settle toward the bottom very slowly and can be worked at an intermediate depth.

The hook point is left exposed with very little difficulty occurring around hangups. The most productive depth is just under the surface where the angler can usually see the bass as it strikes.

The slow, methodical retrieve is much different from the buzzing-type, all-out retrieve of the skimming rig mentioned earlier. Rather than instinctive and impulsive strikes, bass strikes occurring on this rig will be premeditated. The fish will have a moment to think about the wiggling going on in front of its nose before the lure is out of sight.

Floating Worm

Another extremely effective rig is the "floating worm" which is worked on the surface in slow jerks. A high buoyancy worm in a seven or eight-inch length is preferred and is used in conjunction with a light, gold-plated wire

Surface worms can be effective over hydrilla which grows right up to the surface or over eel grass which never quite makes it. Both types make bass territory, however, and the surface worms are the way to reap those benefits. The weedless varieties can be worked well in emergent type of cover such as sawgrass, bulrushes and pepper grass.

hook (2/0 size). This combination will float well on the surface and is deadly.

Sometimes termed the "Florida-rig", it can be snaked slowly across the surface and stopped periodically to lie motionless. The hook should be imbedded in the worm Texas-style when fishing heavy cover. It can be positioned farther down the worm's body than most rigs and adds to its balance. Unlike the other rigs, the hook eye and knot are not exposed.

Large crappie hooks can be used, but if you're expecting large bass, keep the tackle in mind when you have one on and play her accordingly. It is very easy to see the strike with this rig and a novice might find it more successful than the conventional slip-sinker rig for that reason. A surface explosion is always exciting. Bass smash and inhale the worm with mouth open and gills flared, and if they miss, they'll be back after it.

Some experienced anglers add a small float to increase buoyancy. The float can be carved to the desired shape and

SURFACE WORM RIG CHART

Rig	Worm Length	Hook	Rigged	Action	Depths
1. Skimming	9 or 10	4/0 offset worm	Self-Weedless	Fast Buzzing	Surface
2. Swimming	6	No. 2 Straight Shank Bait	Threaded Hook through bend *	Steady Retrieve	1" - 2'
3. Suspended	7¼ or 8	3/0 Straight Worm	Threaded Shank	Slow Jerks	3" - 3'
4. Floating	7¼ or 8	2/0 light wire	Threaded Shank	Jerks and Twitches	Surface

* A swivel should be used 12 inches in front of the hook to prevent line twist

If an angler enjoys seeing the strike on or near the surface, and also having a livewell full of fish, one of these methods should help. I've included a chart showing the four surface worm rigs, the components and action that I prefer to use with each. Try one or all of them, varying the retrieve, until you can establish the best method for the day. When you do find it, I guarantee you action like you have never seen!

the line threaded through a pinhole before tying on the hook. Styrofoam implants can also be used to add buoyancy to the rig. Bass will often take this rig deep, making the percentage of strikes missed small.

Belly Rig

An unusual rig is tossed successfully by Lake Panasoffkee (Florida) anglers. Guide Del Goodwin tosses a 7-inch black/grape worm over heavy hydrilla growth. "An Eagle Claw, Style 40 hook (5/0) is the only one I've found that won't twist your line, hooking the worm like this," points out Del.

The soft, floating worm is hooked right through the diameter of the worm, at a point midway down from the head. The hook, with 'draped' worm is cast without weight, out over the eel grass and hydrilla beds and slowly reeled back to the boat. If the worm is hooked through the middle correctly, the retrieve will not cause the line to twist.

Surprisingly, this rig with hook point exposed will seldom grab the submerged weeds and hang up. This worm rig was responsible for Del taking a limit of 10 bass that weighed 75 pounds from the Jumper Creek area, a couple of miles west of the lake, off of the Withlacoochee River.

Texas Rig

The famous slip-sinker worm rig is the most popular of all the variations. It is a self-weedless rig (the hook point is turned into the worm) developed for those anglers fishing heavy cover. Bullet shaped sinkers of various sizes are used for depth control. The action of the worm and the angler's sensitivity are enhanced by use of the lighter weights. The bass will feel less drag with a 1/16 ounce weight than with 1/2 ounce sinker in front of the enticing worm.

A soft, floating worm with a swimming-type tail is most

effective when rigged Texas-style. Shorter worm lengths are used in clear waters with little vegetation, or during springtime jaunts after lock-jaw bass. The six-inch size is normally used in and around structure. Longer worms are favorite big bass producers in heavy cover. Even gigantic 11 to 13-inch long "snakes" rigged Texas-style are successful baits for behemoth largemouth in southern waters.

Carolina Rig

This rig is often used for deep water bass. The worm is rigged self-weedless at the terminal end of a 24-inch leader. The connection between the leader and main line is a Sampo ball-bearing swivel which also acts as a stop for the sliding sinker placed above. The worm should be a super-buoyant variety or have the addition of styrofoam-chip implants.

The weights can be bullet or egg-shaped and normally run one-half to three-quarters of an ounce. The heavy sinker is used to get the worm down, to depths beyond 20 feet and keep it there. The floating worm is buoyant enough to float over obstacles. If little cover exists, the hook can be left exposed.

This rig is most often used along deep, submerged islands or humps during the hottest summer days. Due to the bass feeling the heavy weight drag, a quick hook set is recommended when fishing the "Carolina rig". This rig is a productive option.

Other Weighted Rigs

There are numerous other ways to rig a plastic worm that are effective on bass under certain conditions. The jig-

Cast a Texas-rigged worm at the edge of the pad cover and attempt to hit on top of a plant on the perimeter. The weighted worm should ideally bounce on top of the plant and fall between it and another. Bass will normally pick up the worm as it descends.

and-worm combo is deadly in waters with relatively clean bottom conditions. Various types of jig heads may be employed, such as the round, bullet shape, or standup. The latter allows the worm to float upward for greater visibility to the bass. Professional anglers, such as Spence Petros (Fishing Facts Managing Editor), claim that this type of head results in a higher percentage of hooked fish than the regular type jig head.

The worm can be strung on various weedless-type jig heads, such as those with wire or nylon weed guards. The worm can be rigged self-weedless on a jig head, similar to the Texas-rigging when fished in submerged 'jungles'. A small split shot can be added either forward of the hook some 12 inches, or right to the hook, pinched on at the bend (when rigged self-weedless). The weighted worm rigs allow you to fish faster and deeper than those without a weight.

The plastic worm is the one lure that most great bass anglers would put in their pockets if they could carry only one. It can be rigged and fished dozens of different ways: on the surface, bottom, or in between. It can be made to swim, slither, crawl, die (such as in the dead worm technique), bounce, or buzz. The versatile, snake-like plastic can even be used as a trailer on spoons, spinner baits, or crank baits. The limits of its use are probably, to date, not totally defined.

KING OF LIVE BAITS
Shine For Lunker Bass

"**M**Y CORK'S UNDER!" yelled one of my partners, who began to feed out the 25-pound monofilament from the level-wind reel. "I've got one running with mine too," shouted Lon Maas, as he quickly moved to the rear deck to grab his casting outfit, appropriately set on free-spool.

A strong surge on my free-lined shiner at the same time made the excitement individualized. My casting spool blurred with the boat's continued drift and the bass heading the opposite way with her morsel. "We're in a school," I said, scrambing to my feet ready for the hook set.

My fishing partners engaged their reels and snapped their rods back to set the steel hooks into the bass jaws. I followed suit, and we all three had bass on. Lon's bass broke the white-capped surface to the left as the other one shot toward the sky, about 40 yards out between Mass' fish and mine.

The guide's bass, a small 3 pounder, surfaced again and freed herself of the 7/0 weedless, lip jewelry. The other fish hit the waves again and scooted off to the right, toward the front of the boat. My bass finally boiled the surface

*When fighting big deep-water largemouth, it's imperative to keep a
tight line on the hooked fish and move it to the boat quickly. The St.
Johns River twists and turns, forming lunker-laden outer bends.
Guide Lon Maas inspects such areas for additional cover which usually
harbors 10 pound bass. Here, he nets one for the author.*

as I battled her toward the front casting platform. She
then headed to the left, crossing over the second fish still
being fought. My fishing partner quickly ducked as I
positioned myself to the back casting platform to continue
the combat.

"Flip your bass into the boat," instructed Maas. My fish
wallowed on the surface, just 12 feet out, and an excited

Maas grabbed the other line and threw a four-pound bass over the gunwale. His net was clear and ready for my lunker, a fat eight and one-quarter pound largemouth. Action with large native shiners is often like that. We were fishing for some 'deep water' bass on Orange Lake. Our companions that day were guides Dan Thurmond and his wife Betty. They also run the Sportsman's Corner Restaurant and Bait Shop. River shiners up to 12 inches are normally in stock, and their guide boat's bait well will hold 10 dozen for a very long day's fishing. The Thurmonds do change bait often, just as soon as the shiner tires or is struck at and mouthed by a largemouth. Lively bait is essential to pulling their fish from the depths.

Guide bookings for both Betty and Dan are handled through their restaurant and tackle shop at Orange Spring, Florida. The huge native shiners are sold daily, but reservations are a must to secure any on most days. Anglers make reservations for their daily shiner needs months in advance.

Wild Bookings

"Our wild shiners are booked further ahead than the Holiday Inn," Betty quips. "We sell out of our stock each day. I put my name on the calendar for six dozen almost every day of the period from November through May."

Having the shiner concession and guiding does have some drawbacks, however. Dan often has to get bait from the shop tanks and load his boats' live wells at 4 a.m., before anglers begin to arrive. If they spot five dozen shiners in the tanks, which the Thurmonds have reserved for themselves, it's a very difficult situation to get out of gracefully. Once they get the bait out of the tanks however, people won't request them.

We were joined by the Thurmonds in dragging king-sized shiners over an 'apparent' flat on the west shore. As the two boats drifted some 100 yards apart with a 20 mile per

For tight-lining, the Thurmonds hook their large 8 to 12 inch shiners through the lower part of the tail section, just behind the anal fin. They can more easily guide the bait back under the heavy stuff, with this hooking method. "You have to swim your shiner back 20 feet from the edge of the cover to get a strike," says Dan Thurmond, "otherwise, forget it!"

hour wind pushing, we had the three fish on. "Most of the water surrounding that point is 6 feet, but an 8-feet hole runs along here," Betty said. "It's hard to detect with some depth flashers, but the bass know how to find it. Dan's caught and released five bass over 10 pounds just off that point in the last two weeks," says Betty.

The Thurmonds, like most big bass guides primarily fish large river shiners, because most of their customers want to catch trophies, and there is no better bait in this world. While clients have caught several up to 14 pounds, both Dan's and Betty's largest, to date, are just short of that mark. Their biggest have been caught from Rodman Reservoir, Orange Lake, and Half Moon Lake.

Water Maneuvers

The Thurmonds drift their bait in specific patterns. Four rigs are employed to cover the maximum area, but hooking of the bait must be precise to prevent entanglements. Shiners are hooked through either the right or left nostril for the outer rigs and through the lips and out between the nostrils for those rigs positioned mid-boat. Except in certain instances, this keeps the shiners apart and maximizes the water coverage.

The hook is set within three to five seconds after the strike, quicker now than they used to, because it allows for healthier releases. Waiting to set the hook until after the first run stops, results in swallowed bait and hooks. If the fish grabs the baitfish and comes at the boat, that is an exception to the Thurmond's "three second rule." They will wait until the bass runs under the craft and starts moving away from the boat.

"I may miss a few more bass by setting the hook so quickly, but I don't hook them deep this way, regardless of shiner size," says Betty. "We release all our big bass and suggest that our clients only keep what they want to mount."

Betty's most exciting time fishing shiners occurred when she caught a 9 pound, 9 ounce bass from Orange Creek. She put that one in the bait well, brought it home to show it off, and then took it back for release. The novelty of such a catch lies in the characteristics of the little creek. Flowage from Orange Lake moves along the twisting eight-foot wide watershed into Rodman Reservoir, or Lake Oklawaha, as its known by some.

The creek is barely navigable and the creek depth runs from two feet down to six or so. The water is tannic acid stained which helps since the short creek runs and fast current flow dictate fishing literally beside the boat. She hooked the big fish in the confined area and successfully battled it into the boat. The frantic moments of the struggle were well worth it.

Hooking Procedure

To keep lunker bass from getting off, sharpen the hook every time it goes into a shiner or comes out of a bass. Hone the hook and check the line for frays each time the rig is in the boat.

Hooking the wild baitfish appropriately will aid in ease of control and hook set. Most guides prefer to hook the shiner under the anal fin, when 'running' the baitfish under hyacinths or pennywort. The shiner has more power to swim under the floating cover and has a tendency to swim downward, away from the hair-like root structure entanglements.

In heavy cover, such as lily pads or spatterdock, the bait is hooked through both lips in order to keep it free of hang-ups. While some guides prefer to fish floating vegetation, most will admit that a mixture of cover is best for big bass. Hyacinths with a few lily pads mixed in, provide the best structure. While hooks through the shiners' lips are used for those toting floats, steel implants through the back near the dorsal fin are recommended for those shiners dragging only the line and hook into the productive depths.

Line testing 14 to 30 pounds and 7 foot rods with level-winds are choice tackle. Maas, a custom rod builder has found increasing applications for heavier 'shiner-fishing' type rods, since moving to Florida in 1978. Like most guides, Maas generally has his clients use corks when fishing shiners. "They're easier to see," he says. The baits are cast underhand, to land softly near the cover. The bass guides allow the rigged shiner to freely roam the area along the cover. The bobber should be 1-3/4 to 2 inches in diameter and sized to allow the shiner to pull it under only when expending full energy.

To keep lunker bass from getting off, sharpen the hook every time it goes into a shiner or comes out of a bass. Hooking the wild baitfish appropriately will aid in ease of control and hook set.

The relationship between the hyacinth and the structure below is the prime concern to many successful bass anglers. Points that are formed by the plant as well as cuts through them can be productive. John Mc-Clanahan notches the hyacinth line for ease of bait placement.

Shiner Control

"Control of the shiner is the key to catching large bass in lakes with heavy aquatic plant life," says retired Florida guide John McClanahan. "Once the shiner swims back under the pennywort or hyacinth, he's in big bass territory, so hang on to the rod." The man ought to know. Several hundred bass bettering the 10 pound mark for his clients, testify to that. And a 13¼ pound personal best and a 14 pound, 2 ounce client record adds further credence to his accomplishments.

McClanahan amassed impressive bass fishing statistics in the 1970's through use of a highly developed technique to lure lunker largemouth out from under heavy cover. The shiner is a genuine 'tool' to this 'mechanic' who can make that bait fish respond in the manner he wishes. He skillfully directs the shiner into and under the heavy floating vegetation time after time to put some very large bass in the boat.

"The bass will take the shiner head first and move off with it," says McClanahan. "They'll try to hit the bait right behind the head, and if the largemouth doesn't hit it just right, she'll blow it out; if the bass gets a weed with the shiner, she will blow it out."

One of McClanahan's most productive ploys in capturing bass from hyacinth or pennywort is to 'notch' the weed line. He will use his paddle to scoop out small pockets back into the floating weed beds. This will leave the outer edge of the bed full of convenient pockets into which a shiner can swim. The shiner can be allowed to deeper infiltrate the bass territory, while the angler still has sufficient and vital control.

The 'undercover' method of catching bass is not limited to certain hours of the day or to specific times of the year. McClanahan has used the technique to take three bass over ten pounds during one day's fishing and has had an equally successful time using it to take three during one night's fishing. His preferred depth for big bass is nine to eleven feet, day or night.

Moving Water

Shiners definitely take their toll of huge bass in 'current' environments and a guide with very few peers on such waters is Bob Stonewater of the Slab Slinger Guide Service in Orange City, Florida. The man has hundreds of trophy bass taken from the St. Johns River on large river shiners.

There are still lunker bass in deep river water, according to the 36-year old guide and proprietor of the Lunker Hole Fishing Headquarters. But those moving into the shallows during springtime are extremely susceptible to anglers, at a time when they should be left alone to carry

Guide Bob Stonewater is a proponent of the unusual ideology, that of deep water bass angling in the prime spring spawning months. He doesn't believe in fishing bedding bass nor in keeping the big bass that he frequently catches.

out their duties. Stonewater does fine on deep water bass during the spring. His personal one-day best of six bass weighing 55 pounds attests to that.

The St. Johns, like many bass rivers throughout the country, twists and turns, forming outer bends that are deeper than the rest of the river. These are the areas that are inspected by Stonewater for another vital parameter, that is, the strategic position of floating aquatic plants such as hyacinths, pennywort, or millfoil. Some must be present in a deep water bend, or lunker bass just won't be in close proximity, the guide feels.

The shiners are fished one of two ways, either five feet under a cork or freelined into the hole from the anchored boat. Hooks ranging from 5/0 to 7/0 and supporting a wire weedguard, are sized according to the length of shiner. As the baits become exicited, they will frantically struggle toward an exit. Often they will head to the surface only to find out that they can't fly and that their predator is right on their tails. A nervous shiner may swim several feet away to avoid a fatal confrontation with a lunker bass. The observant angler should place the bait right back in the same area that it was spooked from, for maximum action.

Big bass feed in areas near safety, and to them, that is deep water, eight to 12 feet. Rather than wait for the lunkers to move into the shallows to feed, Stonewater goes after them in the closest deep water to the prime feeding flats. He catches them too, and just as quickly releases them. Stonewater, like most of the shiner-throwing guides in the south support and strongly recommend use of the catch-and-release system that's so important in "Big Bass Futures".

Methods Vary

There are several methods for using live shiners effectively for lunker bass: 1) top water wade fishing; 2) dead line; 3) drift (wind aided); 4) controlled drift (with electric motor); and 5) floating dead shiner (chum). Selection and employment of each depends on the time of year and upon the water characteristics. One of these normally works on any given day, and often, two or more may produce the action desired.

The Incredible Shiner Fisherman! That would be more like it. My 12-year-old daughter had just told Vern Fulmer that she thought that he could be related to the Incredible Hulk, of TV fame.

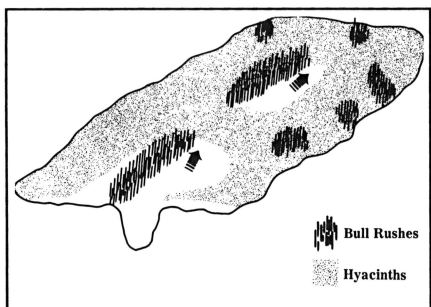

Bull Rushes

Hyacinths

FIGURE-Top Shiner Spot For Lunker Bass

The open waters to the right of the rushes should be productive areas in which to swim shiners back under the hyacinth cover. The line of rushes denote a possible drop off or break while the open water may reveal the presence of a current which has swept away the floating hyacinths. Knowing how to read such potential 'hot spots' can result in putting the bait in the right place to garner some nice bass.

We were sharing a boat with the man, on a small south Florida lake and had amassed a sizable catch of largemouth bass. The husky weight lifter had been revealing his successful shiner fishing methods to me. Fulmer's bermuda shorts and barefeet may have inspired Angela's comment, but the muscular guide, for sure, proved his capabilities as a top lunker bass angler.

His record of accomplishments on big wall-hangers in just the past three years speaks for itself. He has averaged one seven-pound or better bass for each two days spent on

Level-wind tackle with 17 to 25-pound test line, small rubber-core sinker and kahle hook through the shiner's dorsal, is most suitable for 'penned up' bass. Once a concentration of nice sized largemouth is discovered, both ends of the boat must be anchored securely. Then, ready yourself for the action.

the water during that period. In the first 5 months of 1981, Fulmer and his clients caught 841 bass of which 775 were released. The fish ranged to over 13 pounds and included 19 over the ten pound lunker mark. Fifty-two of the 68 heavyweights that he took, which were over seven pounds, were released.

In March of 1981, the 26-year old guide, with friends Mike Pfiefer and Jerry Harrison, caught on one day, 55 bass over 5 pounds! Seventeen of those Lake Okeechobee largemouth were over seven pounds. This catch provided Fulmer with the necessary inspiration to turn to guiding as a full time profession. Since then, he and Pfiefer have had another impressive string of twenty bass, which weighed 155 pounds, almost an eight-pound average!

Surface Action

Originator of the top water, wade-fishing method, Fulmer utilizes it extensively in and around the bullrush beds on Okeechobee. He normally wade-fishes with rather unique shiner fishing gear, an eight foot rod and bait casting reel filled with No. 6 or No. 7 level-floating fly line. The rig is completed with a 3/0 to 5/0 Kahle hook tied directly to an 18-inch, 30 pound test monofilament leader with a small bobber affixed about two feet above the bait.

The fly line stays relatively close to the surface, allowing the angler to follow the direction of movement. This facilitates a straight hook set. The float should be matched to the size of the shiner. It should be sized to be effective at holding the baitfish close to the surface, so that the angler can manipulate its movement in the cover.

The best location to toss the shiner is dependent on the time of year, according to Fulmer. The pre-spawn period finds big sow bass in four or five feet of water around forage-holding cover. Bullrush beds grow on hard bottoms and offer irregular growth patterns from which the bass can ambush their prey. Fulmer had his most memorable day (mentioned previously) using this method under such conditions.

Post-spawn activity finds the big bass back in heavier cover and in a less aggressive mood. Concentrations of huge bass are more difficult to find and wade-fish in the summer and fall months, Fulmer believes. Individuals can still be found in bullrush cover, however.

Once positioned about ten yards from the fish-holding vegetation, Fulmer utilizes a two-handed, swing cast of the bait for ease of entry. The tail-hooked shiner should land softly within 12 inches of the cover. Once it enters the water, Fulmer strips one to three feet of fly line with his left hand. The spool is not engaged since a bass will often take a bait, swim off against the drag, feel the tension and drop the shiner.

The shiner is manipulated into all pockets in the cover that are adjacent to open water. A slight pull of the stripped line should keep the bait from burying into the vegetation. The shiner must remain next to the cover for maximum action. Fresh baits which cause a lot of commotion are prime for big bass. Let the shiner 'flutter' on the edge, six to eight inches away from the rushes, for maximum action.

Vegetation Lunkers

On lakes loaded with coontail moss or hydrilla, bass seldom migrate to the shallows to feed. Holes in the coontail out from shore are ideal, however, and make for a great night-fishing lake. On lakes with little heavy cover, most guides will fish closer to the shoreline at night. At times, successful trophy hunters may 'pull' shiners (with bobber attached) to give them needed night action. Pulling or slowly trolling the bait fish along ridges or shelves with the electric motor is also an effective daytime tactic when some additional movement is required to find the bass.

Most accomplished lunker hunters normally move on to another area if they haven't seen any action within 20 or 30 minutes. Areas that were previously productive are given the latter time allowance, while others generally warrant the lessor period. Moving frequently is often required to find a concentration of big bass, and a good healthy supply of bait is a must.

The larger, 8 to 10 inch shiners are the hardiest and will last longer in the bait well or on the hook. The bigger shiners are slower and easier to catch. They are a soft-rayed (finned) fish and relatively easy for the bass to swallow. These traits make them an ideal bait.

The cold-weather lunker catches on shiners normally continue into the summer and fall and several of the methods mentioned will produce. Deep water, shiner fishing techniques work well year around, even in the spring, when most other anglers are covering up the shallows and disturbing the bass spawning activities.

All the guides mentioned are very conservation-minded when it comes to the lunker bass resource. It's their life, and they don't want any part in "messing up" the future of bass fishing. They release their big largemouth, keeping only an occasional one that is injured without favorable chances of survival. And, with all of them doing more than their share of catching big bass on the "King of Live Baits", it's nice to know that they also release their trophies for another to fight.

IV.
BETTER BASS
ANGLING STRATEGIES

AQUATIC VEGETATION
The Right Cover For Food

SHALLOW WATER VEGETATION holds abundant forage, but it can pose particular problems to many anglers. To some, fishing snag-infested waters is as aggravating as trying to sleep outdoors with a swarm of mosquitoes buzzing your ear. Many anglers are afraid to cast into the middle of the stuff and feel that they would lose any sizable bass that they might get on. But, for those that learn how to effectively fish such terrain as hydrilla, water hyacinths, and coontail moss, rewards can be great.

Aquatic weed life offers shelter for fish food organisms, shade, and more comfortable water temperatures for light-shy fish. They may also function as a trap for excess nutrients in over-enriched waters, but this is not usually the case.

Bass chase after forage in heavy aquatic growth, and knowing how to fish such areas to prevent most hang-ups is vital. Shallow weeds and pads generally hold bass, at least for a short time each day. When the feeding movement has stopped, most bass will migrate back to deeper structure. Weeds in deeper waters may, however, provide the bass a sanctuary all day long, under the right circumstances.

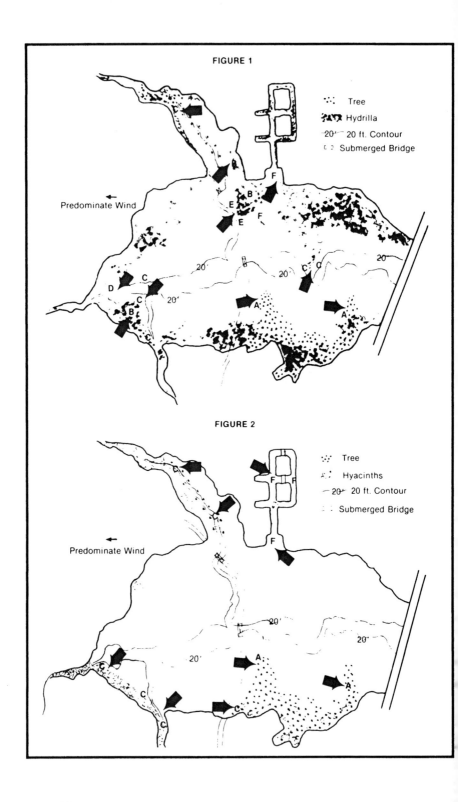

FIGURE 1

Tree
Hydrilla
20' 20 ft. Contour
Submerged Bridge

Predominate Wind

FIGURE 2

Tree
Hyacinths
20' 20 ft. Contour
Submerged Bridge

Predominate Wind

Sorting Out Weed Problems

Locating good areas to fish in lakes that are full of hydrilla or hyacinths can often be a problem. It just all looks the same! Or does it?

The angler should look closer, at the overall picture and try to establish the most potentially productive areas in a body of water. Careful study of a typical southern lake may provide some answers to the most common questions on finding bass.

Figures show what might be typical cover on a lowland reservoir if hydrilla and hyacinth, respectively, were present. Canals, roadbed, submerged trees, and the 20 feet deep contour are shown for reference. The predominant wind direction is delineated for a very important reason: it dictates the areas that hyacinths will blow to and 'stack up'. The tributaries have a minimal current which effects both hyacinth and hydrilla location to a small extent.

The following letters denote potentially productive areas and are applicable for both Figures. An explanation is given for each area:

LOCATION A - Trees forming a point with the presence of either plant should provide good angling. Fish plastic worms along the weed line in the trees and concentrate on the points early and late in the day.

LOCATION B - Small pockets and holes in the weed mat can be productive all day long. A floating minnow imitator twitched over such a hole can provide the best action. The hotter the day, the deeper the bass are in the thick stuff and the slower the lure should be moved to entice them out.

LOCATION C - If a quick drop or 'break' occurs at the edge of a weed line, fish it. Plastic worms and deep running crank baits (crayfish color) are ideal for such structure. Weed entanglements should be at a minimum in such areas.

LOCATION D - This is similar to "C" in that the drop is adjacent to the weedline. The old pond bed that is present may have additional structure which adds interest to this prime worm and top water (protected from wind) spot.

LOCATION E - What may be the best area in the lake is at the point where the submerged road bed lies immediately between the old river channel and a large weed bed. Good deep water structure fishing with worms, jig-and-eels, and crank baits could exist.

LOCATION F - Boat cuts, canal entrances, and other clear water runs are super places for top water and small spinner baits. Any channels through the thick stuff made by current or wave action, or boats can harbor feeding bass in their quieter moments.

During the spring, I've found many fish inhabiting shallow weed beds in the lakes that I've fished. Of course, spawning activity is the ultimate purpose for bass being there, but once the bedding is finished, they can still be found shallow for some duration of time, depending on food availability and water clarity.

Shallow weeds in clear, deep lakes may not hold fish for long, while a stained lake may have the post-spawners for three to six weeks after their love-making duties are complete. A fairly deep reservoir like West Point near the Georgia/Alabama line which is usually clear, will lose the shallow weed-bound bass shortly after spawning. They will move back to the roadbed structure, flooded graveyards, and other excellent deep water structure that the lake contains.

Thickness Of Cover

The length of stay of post spawning bass in shallow waters depends on the density of the aquatic weed cover in addition to the forage availability and water clarity. The more weedy the water, the better its chance of holding a good population of food and bass. Also, the shallower the lake, the more apt bass will be to take up residence in the thickest bed of lily pads or bullrushes available.

Most of the weedy natural lakes in the deep south have shallow-water inhabitants for four or five weeks after the spawn. On Florida's Kissimmee chain of lakes, bass will move from shallow two foot beds to heavy vegetation in about three feet of water and go on a post-spawn feeding binge for a couple of weeks. Then they'll move to the edges of the heavy weed beds (in four to five feet of water) in ambush position and remain there for a few weeks prior to moving to any deeper-water structure that may be present.

Lakes full of deep-water structure and very little shoreline vegetation, such as the clear Table Rock and Bull Shoals lakes in the Ozarks, will have the usual feeding migration, but seldom will many schools of bass be found

As the summer progresses, bass move deeper into the aquatic plants after food and shade. The surrounding presence of huge elephant ears and other vegetation simply provides the best cover in the world for fingerlings to escape predators.

shallow for more than a few hours each day. There is simply not enough shallow vegetation to overcome the clear water and excellent nearby deep water structure.

Weed infested waters can be found all over the U.S., however. I have fished several lakes in Oklahoma and Kansas with an abundance of aquatic vegetation. Angling in Minnesota, Colorado, Missouri, South Carolina, and Tennessee has shown me that fishermen in those states have their share of weed beds. The winter weather can knock the weeds down quickly, but they'll come again in the spring or early summer.

Weather Influences

More than once I've gone back to a location where a huge bed of bonnets had existed the fall before, only to find the April day just too early for the midwestern lily pads. Consequently, some of the better weed fishing can be had in the late spring, just after the spawn.

If the winter weather 'eases into' spring, then normal spawning activity and vegetation growth will occur simultaneously and bass will have adequate holding cover for post-spawn. If spring rushes in, a few hot days could put the urge in the bass, but a lag of the weed growth could preclude any heavy bass foraging and the resultant fantastic shallow-water weed fishing.

In some southern states, weed growth is present most of the year. A mild winter increases the possibility of year-around weed fishing. In some states however, the best time to fish the dense vegetation is in the spring and at the latest, early summer. After that, the weed 'blanket' is just too much to penetrate with a lure.

Reading the water in the summer or winter may involve more thought than many anglers wish to spend, and some apparently stop thinking when they step into the boat. Today's successful anglers must know the various kinds of aquatic vegetation and the important differences between them.

A typical lake might contain lily pads, reeds, bullrushes. hyacinths, hydrilla, cabbage, cabomba, milfoil, and pennywort, and knowing the usual relationship between each, can 'clue in' the thinking angler to a pattern at times.

The infamous water hyacinth spread across southern waters, since it's introduction in 1884 from South America. The equally notorious hydrilla has spread to states all over the country and is not limited to only the Sun Belt states. Leaders in the so-called "noxious weed revolution", these two exotics can be troublesome to anglers.

The plants' impact on the environment, contrary to some opinions, is a positive one. Although they often clog up canals and other tributaries, which makes navigation impossible, there are advantages to their presence. They attract and hold enormous quantities of forage. Bass are there too, so the smart anglers are learning how to fish such places.

Lily Pads

Lily pads are generally found in shallow water and only hold fish for a limited amount of time in the summer. These plants grow from mud soil and usually contain forage for longer periods in the fall or late spring. Some varieties of pads are killed off by cold and are of no consequence to the predator/prey relationship in the winter or early spring.

The really big bass love the 'canopy' cover that pads provide and there are actually three or four varieties with which anglers should be concerned. The dollar bonnet can be dismissed as being a very shallow water pad of little value to bass chasers. The lotus, spatterdock, and fragrant water lily should all be of interest though, and a basic knowledge of each may enable the angler to be more successful.

The most common pads may be the tall and dense spatterdocks. Their leaves are oval-shaped and notorious for hang ups, and their flowers are yellow. They exist in lakes, rivers, and canals and prefer waters of high acidity. They protrude out of the water more than the lotus or fragrant water lily and, in doing so, attract more bugs to their stems beneath overlapping pads. The insects in turn bring forage fish and ultimately the bass.

The fragrant water lily bed also harbors multitudes of bugs in its overlapping leaves, which draw shellcracker and bream to the action. This lily has a white blossom and a round leaf that normally lies on the water's surface. The insects travel on top of the pads and are literally sucked right through the leaf by sharp-eyed bream. Look for small 'pin holes' in these pads to determine if bass forage may be present. If bream are numerous in these beds, then bass will be near.

In the late spring, look for lotus shoots to produce good bass opportunities. The winter cold usually kills off the lotus, but it comes back each year in March or April. The new shoots seem to attract the freshly hatched bugs and the resulting food chain.

Floating Cover

The water hyacinth, Eichornia crassipes, has broad, shiny, dark green leaves and bluish-white flowers. A single plant is capable of producing 50 thousand new plants each year. Its shallow draft (root structure) allows the floating hyacinth to blow into and clog almost any shallow area or deeper water with something like trees to contain it. Current or wind will keep some waters clear of the aquatic plant, but some 'boundaries' will hold the hyacinths for years.

The edges of a creek, flooded timber, deep-based lily pads, or brush just under the surface can help establish the plant. Fish will hold under such cover much of the year, depending upon the food depth and water temperature. A hyacinth 'blanket' will be loaded with grass shrimp, crayfish, and small minnows, and as such, will hold bass interest longer.

The best areas to search out hyacinth for bass are usually over the deeper waters if there is something there to hold them. Any 'structure on structure' is an excellent fish magnet, so contained hyacinths in flooded trees, heavy grass beds, lily pad fields, or fallen logs are excellent areas to fish.

A few years ago, I was working spinner baits in a small 50-acre lake on a windy day. I noticed some small blackbirds clinging to some reeds on the windward shore as I approached the spot. The hyacinths had blown in and it was hard to hold the boat out, away from the spot, but I made a cast to the edge of the hyacinths.

There was an immediate strike and when I set the hook, I couldn't budge her. She took out line and started to come up under the floating plants. I worked her free of the root entanglement and had a great fight until we could put the net to use. I've caught several larger than the eight pounder, but can't remember a better tussle. The largemouth jumped five times, usually clearing the water, an exciting feat for a large bass.

Bird Traffic

One thing to be aware of is bird traffic. If there are birds feeding and walking around on the floating plants, then there must also be small bugs, worms, etc. in the plants. The older a plant is and the longer it has been in one spot, the more food will be present. Birds are a key to finding some of the better hyacinth jams where large bass may lurk.

Another bass benefit you may discover in these beds is the lunkers eager for a feathered meal. Bass will definitely attack birds when possible, and swirls and splashes beneath birds that are tip-toeing over the hyacinths are common. Usually, they'll miss their targets, but if you're quick, you can get a cast in close to the action and maybe score on the predator.

The insect-hunting birds will tip you off to the bait fish and the bass. Egrets and herons working a bank near a hyacinth jam usually mean minnows are also present and might be working beneath the plants, where the larger fish can get at them. Coots and ibis are frequent feeders in hyacinth jams and birds to watch, although almost any kind of activity around the plants is a good sign.

The pennywort is a floating plant also, but it has a longer root structure which is much more intertwined than the hyacinth. As such, it is much more difficult for the wind or current to move around. It moves as a single mass once it has started to propagate in an area and, once established, seldom relocates.

Due to its inability to blow away from open water or creek channels, the pennywort is often found above good structure or drops. It can and does become established over submerged canals, stream and river beds, and other deep water open areas. The knowledgeable angler that views the weed blankets should be able to determine that the ideal summertime bass fishing would be up next to pennywort which is covering an old creek channel. The surface expression of the aquatic plants tells him that!

In dense weed mats are tiny freshwater shrimp and bugs of all kinds, and some feeding activity does go on after a cold front moves through. To find holes to fish in these mats is sometimes difficult, and many anglers who fish areas such as this have to create their own. Thus, a pitch fork or garden rake can be standard equipment in some boats. They are used to make holes in the floating weed mats and then the openings are jigged with small jigs and jig-and-spinner combinations.

Bullrushes And Reeds

The largest bass are usually found in reeds and bullrushes which are in or near deep water, places where shade can be found. Most consistent lunker bass anglers fish the cattails, bullrushes (buggy whips)) and heavy reeds that comprise aquatic jungles (and bass haunts) everywhere. Many prefer fishing the tall, emergent vegetation rather than grass, hydrilla, and coontail since they feel a worm can be worked more naturally through that cover.

The professional lunker chaser often prefers fishing bullrushes and cattails in five to seven feet of water. They fish points some days, and pockets on others, depending on the pattern established early. They don't waste time in one place if it's not producing.

I was fishing heavy bullrush cover on Lake Cypress in central Florida one sunny afternoon when all of a sudden, a large bluegill shot out from the cover on the surface with a huge wake just behind it. The action, not thirty feet away, continued for several seconds as the chase lasted for about thirty feet.

My partner and I whipped that area to a froth with our lures, to no avail. We worked it slowly for over fifteen minutes trying to hook that fish, evidently a large bass. We finally left and after thirty minutes returned to that spot only to again come up with nothing.

My friend was not about to give up though. After a short run across the lake, and thirty minutes more of fruitless casting, we cranked up to return for one last shot at that fish. He cut the engine and slowly motored us in with his electric trolling motor. His first cast fell perfectly into the bullrush pocket in which the large wake had first appeared. He moved it once, felt a pickup, and came back hard on the rod to set the hook.

The bass shot to the surface, right in the middle of the rushes, and we both knew then that the elusive bluegill-chaser was now on! My partner skillfully worked the large bass from the dense cover and brought her to the boat. I carefully netted the lunker which later weighed in at eight pounds, four ounces, very much worth our extra effort. A good angler seldom gives up on a big bass that is in a feeding mood.

Hydrilla

Hydrilla has only been in this country for 21 years and Lake Conroe in Texas is not unlike many lakes with the plant. It began to develop its 'crop' soon after the reservoir was created. Vast amounts of good structure now lie covered with mats of the noxious week. But, in the same regard, hydrilla has created new 'breaks' and even better defined the lake's existing structure in some chases. A 'weed line' in such lakes, may establish the presence of a quick drop in depth due to a creek bed or river channel.

Several thousands of acres of 'shag carpet' exist on lakes throughout the U.S. and the exotic plant is extremely hard to control. Hydrilla, a rooted plant, can survive in almost any weather and it spreads by fragmentation. Small fragments of hydrilla on a boat trailer can be 'transplanted' from one lake to another, and from state to state. The fragments then root and grow into large plants, thus infiltrating another lake.

Once hydrilla gets a foothold in a 'virgin' lake, it is hard to stop. Wind, waves, and boaters cut and separate the soft, upper shoots of the plant, and it is very competitive, so firm establishment in most waters is a reality. The plant is though to be light independent and shade or water clarity may have little effect on its growth. It will, however, grow to the light once it has been established in the depths.

Although coves are easily choked with the mats of hydrilla, fishing for bass and all other species normally improves. The plant may be a menace during spawning periods if the shallows become clogged, but good spawns normally occur despite the problems. The forage is tremendous in such waters and the fish population actually increases.

Any heavy mass of aquatic plants that grows to the surface of a lake and then mats up and clogs the water is particularly hard to fish. Many varieties of small floating plants or weeds that cover the surface require a special type of lure also.

Surface Observation

The water's surface can also be 'read' even though the hydrilla is not emerging from it. Wave action can tip off the observant angler to bottom conditions and thus, help him determine exactly what is below.

A friend and I were on a small reservoir last spring when a strong southerly wind came up, turning the lake into large swells and white caps. But, upon close observation, we noticed that not all waves were 'breaking' in the same manner. Some were short and choppy, while most were long, and swell-like.

Water weeds, such as hydrilla are notorious aquatic pests, but they do support a fantastic forage base.

The presence of an underwater hump had been detected. Actually, it was the remnants of a spoil dike formed before the flooding of the reservoir. The wind was pushing waves right into it and they were breaking on top of the shallow hump in a relatively deep area of the lake. We assumed that baitfish would also soon be stacked up against the hump, due to the strong winds. Bass could not be far behind, we reasoned, and they were not. Within the hour we boated five largemouth including a six-pounder from the windward side of the hump! The vast aquatic weed cover and the lake's newness to us had hidden the hump's identity, but the strong cuss-worthy winds had uncovered the secret.

Invisible Current

A current to many fish means easier feeding and a cooler, more hospitable environment. To John Mc-Clanahan, a former fishing guide in Orange Springs, Florida, it also means deeper water and bigger bass.

John and I spent a half day touring the upper reaches of Lake Oklawaha (Rodman Reservoir) in north central Florida. We easily stopped at ten places before finding the bass that afternoon. Each small place might have appeared, to a casual observer, as being identical to thousands of other areas nearby. However, one trait existed in the ten spots that we fished, which was not common to the other areas - current!

A glance at each specific location revealed bullrushes or other tall weeds bordering the open water and eel grass abutting it. The long, thin leaves of the submerged grass were flapping in the current. This was obvious as we approached due to the clarity of the water. The entire water was covered with floating water plants, yet the deeper submerged canals and creek beds were loaded with eel grass 'clues'.

Overgrown, floating weed masses with a current moving beneath provide excellent habitat for concentrations of largemouth. Often, the angler must analyze the topography to detect such places.

John and I took fifteen largemouth between two and four pounds from one area that we fished for a little over one hour. This particular portion of an old canal bed was loaded with aquatic weeds and bass. The thousands of acres around it were barren that day, but the surface expression did provide the keys to that 'honey hole'!

FEEDING BASS
Schoolers Are More Catchable

THE SURFACE EXPLODED on two sides of the boat as we frantically whipped our lures into the activity. Bass were everywhere, and small two-inch shad were flying high into the sky. The Orange Lake bass had again pushed the schools of shad up to the floating "islands" and were feasting as though there would be no tomorrow.

My partner and I quickly landed two small keepers and promptly flipped our lures back for more. Three more 14-inch bass were landed before the school disappeared. The shad reformed and again serenely scooted along the surface as though nothing had happened. Our deep running lures produced nothing as we spray-cast the area.

Then, as suddenly as before, bass were again on the surface, in a gorging disposition. We landed three more and hung twice that many while they ran rampant. Again they retired to the depths, for a good forty minutes this time.

Schools of heavyweight bass never really formed on Orange Lake before I had to leave, but we did manage to take several nice largemouth, the biggest around 3½ pounds. After pictures, all were released to once again chase the roaming schools of shad. Unfortunately, we didn't catch any of the lake's 'hawgs' while following the shad schools. Since shad are an open-water species, they are consumed more by the nomadic 12 to 14-inch largemouth than they are by big bass. Largemouth schools will feed on about any kind of schooling forage. Anything they can get their jaws around, they'll put in their mouths. Bite-sized threadfin shad may be the most common forage for the schools of feeding largemouth. They are prolific and can have several spawns a year (usually two), increasing their availability. The gizzard shad is a larger species than its cousin and primarily attracts the monster bass packs.

The action reminded me of similar occurrences that I've experienced throughout the country. In fact, most lakes, including many of the smaller ones, have an adequate supply of forage which 'school up' and provide marauding bass schools with supper, and anglers, enjoyment. The successful angler is always on the lookout for surface activity which might denote feeding fish. There will be some noticeable movement generally when school bass are around. Be prepared, and always cast to any feeder you might spot. If you're quick, you might take three out of every five that you cast to. Remember, casting to a feeding (or active) fish is worth much more than casting to a spot where activity is nonexistent.

Time of day makes a big difference in schooling activity. In general, the dissolved oxygen is at its peak between 4 p.m. and 6 p.m. each day, regardless of the time of year. This 'rule of thumb' is primarily due to the sun's effect and may vary due to other isolated events. Because of this, feeding schools are much more frequent on most lakes during the late afternoon hours.

One very important thing to remember for schooling action is to be close to the wind action. It'll be more difficult to control the boat but it should be worth it. The wind pushes floating vegetation and bait fish to the windward side of the lake or river, and the bass schools won't be far behind.

Honey Hole Schoolers

A couple of years back, I was working some shallow pad fields with little success when my companion, Guy Settlemeyer, decided to forego further early-morning chasing of the lunker bass that we were after. Instead, he took me to a 'honey hole' of his that was loaded with average-sized fish. The ten minute boat trip put us into some submerged timber which, from a casual observation, resembled one thousand other areas on this lake. But, it was different.

A change in depth was not apparent as we slowly moved across two open areas to tie up to a large tree which emerged from the water near several others. The next two hours of fishing from that location was 'slow' according to Guy's standards, fifteen bass between two and three pounds each, and another 25 that averaged around 12 inches. He had been catching double that in his previous four trips to the lake!

The reason the bass were schooling in that area was obvious to both Guy and myself. The treeline was a migration path for feeding largemouth. The path makes a bend at that location and holds bass longer than a straight treeline would. In the middle of the turn is a point of trees which 'separates' the migration into two parts. The fish were at this location for several hours each day, according to Guy, and a mussel bed or other bottom structure was non-existent.

The area provided a good ambush point for the bass, and the heavycover phobia that many open-water forage fish have would aid their movement along (and not into) the trees and to the bends.

The treeline defined the structural paths that the forage and predators moved along, in this case. The trees were, in many cases, only four feet apart, yet to the forage, the treeline may as well have been a brick wall. Small forage schools are usually very reluctant to penetrate such cover, and this trait makes for easier foraging by the largemouth and other gamefish such as the striped bass.

The important thing to remember when you do locate bass on an unusually warm, springlike day is to stay with them. Establish a pattern and hit it hard while you can. Several years ago, my father, mother and I arrived at Minnesota's Lake Lida, just as a warm snap had thawed the area. We pulled into this spot about 3 o'clock in the afternoon and began casting to the bank and retrieving back over the logs. From our first cast on, the bass couldn't be stopped. The warm sun had made the shallows comfortable and the biggest school of bass I'd seen in a long time moved in to feed. All three of us caught maybe 15 bass apiece in one hour without moving the boat, and the action never stopped.

Feeding Routes

The principle that a forest of submerged trees defines a route for food fish and their predators to follow was further demonstrated that afternoon. The location was a 'cut' from a large open water portion of the lake to a smaller, but also open-water area. Flooded trees with floating hyacinths trapped between them established the boundaries.

We had taken four good bass from the cut area earlier in the day but had found no consistent action. The few fish present were feeding in the deep, in some twenty feet of water. A shade line below the floating plants existed in conjunction with the treeline and further helped to prevent encroachment by the forage schools that periodically moved through the cut.

Fishing was relatively slow and the late afternoon sun was heading for the horizon when I suggested to Guy that we move back to the cut. We motored over to it and, as we approached, could hear the ruckus from several large fish that were feeding on prey at the surface. The bass were popping schools of small shad that had been chased and funneled into the cut from the large open-water area.

Schools of trophy bass, larger than I've ever seen, were feeding on top and they seemed to be all over the cut. The action continued for 45 minutes and coincided with a major solunar period that started at 6 p.m. that day. Plenty of schools of five and six pound fish moved after the shad, into and through the one-hundred foot wide cut, but the eight to ten pound bass schooling on top that afternoon were awe inspiring to this angler.

At any one time during that period, there were three to four separate and distinct schools slashing shad on top. Each school had four to eight fish on the surface at all times while they moved through the cut. It .was obvious that the treeline (and hyacinth line) was a boundary in this case.

Shad Blow Up

As the large schools of bass pushed the forage to the edges of the cut, the action would then move back toward the more open water in the center. Many shad were knocked up on top of the hyacinths, but they would not venture back under the floating plants.

Some thirty-five bass were hooked and most were over two pounds. We returned all to the water except three six-

Many school chasers head to the mouths of rivers or other tributaries which are present on many larger ultraclear lakes in the state. The water may be less clear in the tributaries due to the nature of the drainage. Feeding schools will often gather in this deep water area as the river is rising.

pound fish and a couple that were deeply hooked. That action will long be remembered.

Feeding fish like these would hit almost anything resembling a bait fish. A Bill Norman Little "N" crankbait, a Bagley Salty Dog, and a Bagley Small Fry Shad were among the most effective lures in that situation. Top water baits produced surprisingly little.

We had to wonder why, at times, the bass school could be attacking everything close to it, yet not even notice our lures. One extremely critical time that this happened was when two different schools of bass, in the eight-to-ten pound range, were on the surface, bashing the shad schools not thirty feet from the boat. While Guy tossed into the frenzy four or five times without a strike, I was being entertained by a stubborn six-pounder that I just couldn't shake off! I missed the potential for action with a ten pounder.

The 'waves' of schooling bass that moved through the cut that afternoon kept our rods arched and even our arm muscles straining. The action was a vivid reminder of the importance of relating surface expression and forage behavior to the quarry we were seeking.

Live Baiting With Shad

The use of live threadfin shad is perhaps the most deadly method ever devised for taking schooling bass in open water according to Frank Sargeant, southern field editor for "Outdoor Life."

"Bass seem simply unable to turn down a live shad struggling on a hook," he says. "They'll take it in preference to any artificial, and usually in preference to any other live bait."

Regardless, very few anglers actually use the bait. Shad are extremely difficult to keep alive in captivity. The fragile bass prey won't last long on a hook either. After 5 minutes or so on a number 2 hook, they'll wear out and a replacement is required. Thus, a good supply of lively bait is necessary.

They can be captured by tossing a castnet with a small mesh, over a school. A sensitive chart recorder can be used to locate the schools which often hang out just below surface plankton. When the shad schools are on top, they are detected by ripples as they move about. Ease the boat up to them and toss the net over the mass. Low light levels make it easier to sneak up on the bait when they are positioned on or near the surface.

Light line is preferred for fishing these delicate baits and minimal casting is recommended. They are usually fished without weight and hooked similarly to any other forage fish: through the lips, beneath the dorsal fin, and through the tail. The three or four-inch long size is preferred by the successful shad-bait fisherman.

Shad, like shiners, become very nervous when bass swim by. This situation causes frantic behavior of shad, which is easily observed by the angler. The small baitfish begins to swim frantically and often leaps at the surface. The angler should be ready for the impending strike.

Live baiting with shad can provide fast and furious action. Many proponents of their use have caught huge stringers of bass. The best baits are captured right from the waters being fished.

Bass school up in many waters and the best month may vary depending on the area, type of water, and weather conditions. It's action that is generally worth looking out for, and a "schoolie' rod should always be rigged with a shad imitation and be available. You can't always tell when a surface school of shad may 'blow up' next to the boat and an acre of bass inundate the calm.

NOCTURNAL NEWS
The Active Time Of Forage

NIGHTTIME ANGLING IS a unique adventure. You see a commotion in the distance, hear the resounding splash as a bass wallops the lure, set the hook, and then you 'feel' how heavy she is. There's no other way to tell. You can't see proportions of the fish well enough.

Fishing by moonlight is a common occurrence during the summer months, but more and more anglers are enjoying the activity in the spring and fall. Night angling is most productive because the forage is most abundant at this time. The fisherman's mistakes are also covered by the guise of darkness. The predator bass is often less wary or 'spooky' after dark. Their fright often turns to curiosity when the sun goes down.

Bass feed at night for several good reasons. Insects are out and baitfish often cruise just beneath the surface, swiping off a bug every now and then. Bass are not far behind.

You only have to run your boat across a lake at night with a spotlight beam to see and experience the insect life after dark. Once you have scooted through some bug 'storms', you'll be picking them out of your teeth for several minutes when you stop the boat. Both forage fish and bass love these conditions though.

Shallow water bait fish are also at a disadvantage because of their poor night vision. Under bright sunlight conditions, where they feed near the water's surface on plankton, they are often able to avoid the predators, but after dark these baitfish develop a severe case of night blindness. Deeper feeding bass don't. Their eyes are accustomed to the dimmer light level.

Shine your light on the water's surface and you'll probably see hundreds of frogs. They are gourmet forage for bass, as are freshwater eels, waterdogs, and small bullhead catfish that are usually more active upon nightfall.

The other common night active creature in the bass food chain is the crayfish. This is a favorite morsel and it is definitely a nocturnal feeder. They hide under rocks during sunlight hours and explore the bottom after hours. Their incredibly poor eyesight makes them a prime target for the larger, nocturnal-feeding predators.

Water Selection

Lakes full of forage are great places to chase starlight bass, but other parameters are similarly important for finding the best waters. A prime consideration in selecting a lake for after dark angling, is how well you know the waters. Fish only those waters with which you have a complete intimacy.

As the last light begins to fade, look around at landmarks in relation to distant lights. Under a full moon you can see the shoreline, but on a new moon, you are virtually blind without landmarks or artificial light of some sort.

The most productive waters after dark are generally the hardest to fish during daylight. A good night lake often experiences heavy daytime lake pressure or boat traffic. The sunlight activity on such waters continually disturbs the best accessible fishing areas and creates night feeding patterns. After the speed boaters have departed, bass become less wary and are overcome by their hunger.

The shallows that produce small bass in the day often contain lunker bass in the low light. Under the cloak of darkness, bass move out of the dense vegetation into and around the edges of their cover. They'll migrate along the deepest shadows into the shallows where they are more susceptible to the angler's lures.

This ultra-quiet period on a cool, refreshing evening can make the most boat-shy bass forget the daily congestion. Many anglers realize that bass in the heavily fished lakes and rivers become less cautious and move shallower on their feeding migration when the sun goes down. But not too many know just how effective fall fishing at night can be, for big bass.

Small lakes that heat up during a hot day and cool down nicely at night are also prime candidates for good after-dark angling. The cooler temperatures at night not only activate the bass, but they also keep the hordes of fishermen off the water. Usually, clear-water lakes offer better fishing at night than during the day, while a muddy lake may not be more productive. A bass haven whose water resembles something found in a drinking glass should be fished at night, since daytime fish movements are often severely limited.

Many clear water lakes, both large and small, fit into the superior night waters category. Table Rock Lake in Missouri, Bull Shoals Lake in Arkansas, the Hill Country lakes in Texas, Lake Tenkiller and Grand Lake in Oklahoma, Wilson Reservoir in Kansas, Lake Guntersville in Alabama, West Point Lake in Georgia, Santee Cooper in South Carolina, and East Lake Tohopekaliga and Lake Weir in Florida are a few of the excellent waters with night angling reputations, that I have fished. Many others exist throughout the U.S.

Some pretty large bass are taken after dark. The Orange Lake, Florida record bass of 17 pounds, 4 ounces, caught by R.W. Campbell is the largest ever taken on a top water lure. Campbell got a backlash on his very first cast during pre-dawn darkness, spent 15 minutes picking it out, and then barely moved the black Jitterbug. The huge bass sucked it in and took off, only to be subdued.

The last two state record largemouth bass in Kentucky were taken after dark. Del Grizzle caught the current state mark, a 13 pound, 8 ounce, from a very small lake using a plastic worm. He used extreme stealth and tried to inconspicuously cast the worm upon the bank trying not to make a splash. He was amply rewarded on that moonlit night.

Feeding Bass

Locating bass at night is generally easier than during daylight. The shallows that produce small bass in the day, often contain lunker bass in the low light. Under the cloak of darkness, bass move out of the dense vegetation into and around the edges of their cover. They'll migrate along the deepest shadows into the shallows where they are susceptible to the angler's lures. Boat lanes, weedlines,

At night, some bass move along the same routes that they do before dark and many very big ones venture shallower under the guise of darkness. It is a pleasant experience to have some good fish at daybreak and be heading for the house.

timberlines and shallow dock pilings are excellent after dark spots.

I remember my first night fishing trip several years ago. Crickets and frogs roared and explosions on the surface of the calm lake resembled alligators foraging, more so than bass. My eyes hadn't fully adjusted to the darkness when something tried to take away my casting outfit.

The thief, a six pound largemouth, made her way into some submerged timber, but the line held as I bullied her out of the obstruction and toward the boat. The bass took to the sky and sounded like a sure ten-pounder when it descended back into its home territory.

A second jump closer to the net gave me a chance to eyeball the fish. I had momentarily forgotten that things are magnified after dark when an angler must rely on senses other than sight. Somewhat disappointed and over my illusion, I brought her to the boat and my partner placed the bass in the livewell. It was the first of what would be a total of five of similar stature.

We eventually released sixteen additional bass of smaller proportions. We had lots of action that night on Lake Oklawaha in northeast Florida, but the real heavyweights were scarce.

It was a fairly typical night however, for my companion. He had been catching 20 to 30 bass each weekend night during the previous two months, when he suggested that I join him on a 'no-dozer'. While many anglers reach for top-water lures when the sun goes down, we chose to toss the highly productive Texas-rigged worms.

From sundown to 3 a.m., the two of us probed the edges of a 3-foot deep spoil area with black plastic wigglers. The lake's main channel is approximately twenty-feet deep and lies on one side of the spoil area, while an 8-feet deep flat lies on the other. All of our bass came from the top of this "hump", in close proximity to the rapid drop. Weighted worms were bounced down the drop and into the mouths of the bass.

Good drop-offs near shallows, but closest to the deeper waters, are the best nighttime targets. At night, bass will

Darkness brings out the shy bass who normally favor deeper haunts. Fishing mid-depth structure can bring the super hawgs out and a moon can aid the angler's visibility when they are found.

use the same feeding routes they use during the day. How far they'll travel along this route will depend on light, food, and the nature of the structure that guides them. At night we can expect this movement to terminate closer to the shallows than in the daytime. As water temperatures get colder, these movements will be shorter and more abrupt, even at night.

Long bars and submerged points on shallow, clear natural lakes are excellent areas to find congregated bass. Any daytime feeding activity that takes place will probably occur at the end of the bar, but at night the strategy changes. On bright, moon drenched nights, the successful angler has to treat the lunar rays like those of the sun. Bass will hide in the shadows of structure and move along the shaded sides of cover to ambush their prey.

As night sets in, better fish movement may take place along the sides of the bar. A flat with some structure will act as a route for the fish to follow toward shore after they have migrated in along the elevation change. Other features that may be present to make such a spot even better are aquatic growth, which provides cover and food (insects), and an incoming creek with moving water. Baitfish will frequently be found by predator bass at the mouths of tributaries.

Baitfish Magnet

Lighted piers are a magnet to the entire food chain. Vern Fulmer, now a guide on Lake Okeechobee believes in lighted boat docks. While attending a nearby university a few years ago, he spent many evening hours after class, casting to several boat docks on Georgia's Lake Sidney Lanier. Most of the docks have submerged trees which were placed there for crappie.

Fulmer and a classmate were tossing broken back Rapala's on a dark June night when they came upon the only lighted dock in Flowery Branch Cove. They quickly caught two bass and moved in close to take a look. The bass were 'stacked up' in the crystal clear four feet of water beneath the light.

They moved the boat back to a casting position and tossed live, six inch salamanders into the mass. The bait was hooked through the lips with 1/0 weedless hooks and fished without weights in order to keep the landing splash as quiet as possible.

"We caught two or three bass on each salamander," laughs Fulmer. "We would catch the bass on one side of the boat and release them on the other. They would then swim right back to the school."

The two tired anglers finally called it a night at 3 a.m. They had caught forty bass between two and four pounds each from waters supporting Georgia's heaviest boat traffic!

Boat docks with lights are great, but the double-wide boat houses that are painted white are equally productive, according to Doug Hannon. "They are like big movie screens to the bass," says the big bass specialist. The largemouth will seek some source of light or pale colored background to see the outline of their prey.

Collection Areas

"Dark areas collect fish in daylight, light areas attract them on the black nights," adds Hannon. "A white sand beach is a good place to look. Toss a jig out and let it lie on the sand. A bass will move over and pick it up."

Swimmer's feet kick up bottom sediment and forage move in to feed after the wet set have vacated the area. Bass can easily catch their prey over the white sand. My after dark experiences on Missouri's Table Rock Lake have proven this. Some excellent bass strings were taken under the moon from a pebble-laden swimming beach next to a busy marina.

Other areas with a light colored bottom are good night fishing spots. Shallow depressions or holes in heavy vegetation next to the bank, attract huge largemouths under the low light conditions. Doug Hannon's largest

A white sand beach is a good place to look. Swimmer's feet kick up bottom sediment and forage move in to feed after the wet set have vacated the area. Bass can easily catch their prey over the white sand.

nighttime bass came from a small hole in Lake Keystone's hydrilla. It preceded by just two nights his wife's largest bass ever, a 12½ pounder, from the same hole!

Timing Nocturnal Movement

Bass will move around more at night than during daylight hours and they are less dependent on good structure during moonless evenings. Bass can totally utilize an extremely shallow area at night, whereas they may be 'confined' to a deeper, sun-drenched point during the day.

Midnight feeding bass prefer still water and are often in shallow water near a deep water drop-off. Productive fishermen often fish off of the bottom so their lures are silhouetted against the sky. They make short, more controllable casts and they are prepared for the strikes that occur right at the boat. Successful anglers are alert to the grip of the rod and thumb pressure on the reel and are not lulled into a sleepy trance by the mesmerizing gurgle of the moving lure.

Successful night anglers have their own ideas about the best possible time to chase bass. All seasons get votes from the productive nightowls and the optimal time after sundown varies depending on a couple of parameters. There are not as many variables in night angling but temperature and oxygen levels are important.

The basic difference between our eyes and those of a bass is that ours normally adapt from bright to darkness more quickly. While it normally takes human eyes about 30 minutes to fully adapt to darkness, the night vision of a bass could take as long as a few hours in cool water. Summer bass activity peaks earlier after sundown than does winter foraging.

"The water temperature is the most important factor in all of bass fishing," says Hannon. "If the temperature is below 70 degrees, go after midnight."

Bass are more active in hot water as their metabolism increases, but oxygen is also a key to the best time. Dissolved oxygen levels peak toward the end of the day and plants then demand oxygen. Decreasing oxygen levels in the summer are big factors in bass feeding. The lower oxygen in weedbeds after midnight may prohibit extensive activity until dawn. With a substantial reduction in winter plant life, oxygen levels are less of a factor in bass activity.

Guide Elroy Krueger is a firm believer in chasing the night feeding largemouth. The Universal City, Texas angler has caught several limit stringers weighing 50 to 60 pounds from both Lake Braunig and Lake Calaveras. Two of the three largest bass ever taken from Lake Calaveras were also hooked at night. The lake record of 13 pounds, 9 ounces weighed in by Bill Guiliani some 15 hours after it was caught, came on a major period just three nights before the full moon.

Solunar influences have a big impact on night angling. The three nights before a full moon and the three nights after are preferred by many nocturnal fishermen. Experts believe that the biggest bass are caught when the moon comes up before the sun goes down.

Krueger's best nights on Calaveras include three, with half a dozen bass over seven pounds. He caught largemouth over 7 pounds on six successive nights last summer on nearby Lake Braunig, but his best evening on that lake was six bass that weighed 52 pounds.

Night fishing doesn't necessarily mean big stringers, but fortunately, the single-strike night is a rare happening. Nocturnal angling does, however, leave the fisherman with memorable experiences of tranquility and occasionally, the largest bass of his life.

LURE OF THE NIGHT
Proper Tackle Selection Is Essential

When an angler is relying more on touch and sound than on visual contact, the importance of the right tackle, lure, and peripheral equipment is obvious. Proper selection and placement of the necessary items can make late-hour bass fishing both successful and enjoyable.

Since lunker bass are more prone to making mistakes and getting caught after dark, light tackle considerations can go off into the night. Nightime masks need for such gear and lines of 20 to 40 pound test can be easily employed depending on the size of fish sought.

Since noise in shallow water will invariably scare off feeding bass, the use of heavy line may be vital to angling success. The heavier lines will stretch less and can be safely used to pull a lure loose when hung up in thick vegetation.

While several anglers prefer heavy spinning tackle for the pitch-black evenings, the majority of anglers use level wind reels. The new Magnetic Force baitcasting reels have eliminated most of the backlash worry for many users. Most anglers prefer long, stiff-action rods to pry bass out of shallow, weedy cover.

In the lure category, nocturnal bassmen are concerned primarily with silhouettes and vibration, so color is relatively unimportant. Dark lures are preferred by most nightowl bass chasers, since they cast a darker 'shadow'. A black artificial lure should net more results than fishing a live baitfish which is shaded for minimum visibility. Lure type is a more important parameter than color after dark.

Shallow weeds and heavy vegetation are often difficult to see at night, so tangle-free lures are invaluable. The advantages of a single-hook lure over the dual trebles of a large topwater are obvious. The jig and eel, curly-tail plastic lizard and large plastic worm rigs that resemble snakes and other creatures of the night are weedless so you'll spend less time freeing the lure from entanglements. Since many strikes occur at boatside, you'll appreciate the safety there also. Once the fish is in the boat, the lures are easier to remove by flashlight.

A swimmin' worm rig is very productive at night. The weightless lure twists along near the surface, well above the predator bass. It's silhouette outlined against the skylight and smooth movements attract strikes from below.

Blade baits with their thumping, spinner action combined with dark silhouette can maximize weight on starlight stringers. When bass have moved into heavy cover, a buzzing spinner bait running over the weed beds can bring jolting strikes. Crank baits equipped with rattle chambers excell at night in less dense bass habitat.

I'd certainly be remiss if topwater lures were left out of this discussion. In low light conditions, they are difficult to out-produce, but using them exclusively could be a mistake. Surface plugs and moonlight just go together. Tossing the lures at dimly lit targets and hearing the satisfying splat as they touch down is night casting. Hearing the steady rhythm on the retrieve stopped by a loud slurp or a nerve-shattering explosion is night fishing!

The premier topwater plug for sundown times is the Jitterbug. For monster bass, the Musky-size 'Bug' gurgling across the surface can't be beat. Nightime bass anglers worship this plug. They toss it out over heavy cover and count to five after the splash, before starting their retrieve. A slow, steady reeling will excite the biggest of bass which often strike out in anger. If they miss it, they'll often come back after it. Beware of the rod-tip strikes which will test both the tackle and your heart simultaneously.

Although you should attempt to minimize tackle after dark, pre-rig several outfits with a variety of lures to minimize changes. Night bass can be finicky, so have a small arsenal ready for them. When darkness closes in around you, it's wise to keep fumbling to a minimum. During the diminishing daylight, place everything in the proper place. Know where your equipment is!

Never try to lip-lock a brawling bigmouth after dark. Since it's hard to find the treble hooks, use a net. A flashlight with a red lens will preserve your night vision and provide the light for unhooking fish, etc. Red nail polish or red crepe-paper can alter the clear lens, which could also spook the bass. Avoid directing the beam over water or at your partner. The variable intensity Moon Glo Bass Lite throws out enough illumination to adequately light up nearby action without scaring the fish.

WOOD HABITATS
Where Baitfish Congregate

THE SEVEN LAYERS of clothes that I was wearing helped little in the 40 degree January weather that hit Florida. Tucking his ski mask into his snowmobile suit, Bob McCray jammed the throttle forward on the Evinrude and we were soon on plane.

The wind's chill at 40 miles per hour, cut through our clothing to the bone and even watered our eyes, despite protective goggles. I was elated when he slowed and pointed the boat's bow toward a brushy St. Johns River bank.

"We'll try my hawg hole first," Bob said, as he dropped the electric motor over the bow. "I've taken several lunkers off this bank during the year." He explained, "There's a good drop here with submerged logs and trees all along the bottom."

Actually, we were freezing on a stretch of the river just south of Palatka, Florida, in search of some winter-time bass. Bob took off one glove, but I elected to keep on both of mine. We both chose a spinnerbait which we could fish easily and keep somewhat warm while casting, at the same time. We deemed that the continual reeling of a spinnerbait would help us thaw. Bob endowed his black spin-

The surface expression of submerged brush can be a key to finding timber bass in reservoirs and toppled trees beneath can hold the big ones.

nerbait with a six-inch white worm trailer and limbered up his frozen reel.

Actually, I had little interest in fishing in that cold weather until Bob lunged back, setting the hook hard on his fifth cast. The lunker bass rolled behind the fallen tree limbs and dove into them, taking out drag at will. Soon her entanglement was absolute and she could not take out more line, but the 14-pound test monofilament held.

Bob quickly motored over to the snag, keeping a taut line. We feared the worst. He felt constant movement on the terminal end of his line as he strained to work the hawg free. The tree limbs started to emerge from the water as Bob's constant pressure brought them and the fish up toward my waiting net.

I grabbed the limb and gingerly lifted it out of the water with net in hand. The line looked like a bird's nest entwined in and around the limbs, but the lunker's surge was still evident as I continued to lift. Fortunately, the line held and the bass rolled to the surface. I quickly scooped her up and flipped her into the boat.

Nine pounds and six ounces was a good way to warm up on that bitter, cold morning. We finished that day with three bass each from the submerged logs, but very few other anglers caught anything at all in the 40-degree weather.

Brush and wood habitats provide cover, protection, and food for bass and they can have an influence on water temperature and current flow. Submerged timber in the form of limbs or wood pilings can be found in most lakes and rivers, whether they are man-made reservoirs or natural bodies.

Timber areas, to boost fishery production, have been left standing in most reservoirs constructed in the past ten years for fish management purposes. These areas can be spotted emerging from the water's surface or found with the aid of a map and a good depth finder if they are totally submerged. Natural waters may also have vast areas of submerged brush.

Natural Creek Brush

There are certain areas that almost always have a good brushy bottom. Forage-attracting timber is usually piled in the outer bends of river or creek channels. The constant current slowly erodes the bank and eventually washes away the root-bound dirt. Trees then topple into the deep water and fall, or are washed, to the bottom. As the bank caves in, the channel is widened with the deeper water still on the outer bend. The newly submerged timber lying in the bend, then attracts food fish and bass.

A common cause of timbered bottoms in a lake or river is wind. Hurricanes or tornadoes can knock down multitudes of water-lined trees, and high winds of less magnitude can even destroy many trees.

Toppled Trees

For an angler with a careful eye, it is easy to look at the expression of the trees on shore and determine whether the possibility of submerged structure exists (in the form of brush or timber). Wind-downed trees on many banks are vivid evidence. On the very deep bends, these wind-toppled trees are magnets for forage and bass. It is possible to find a bass hotel in a well-branched, submerged tree and taking several fish from one spot can be exciting.

Other bass-holding timber of prime importance is the root system of fallen trees which will many times appear partially above the surface. Deep shorelines, with plentiful root structure, appear on most river or creek channels and are most prevalent in the low, wind-affected areas.

Root structures are often the only 'wet' part of the fallen tree. The tree will be blown down and fall onto the bank and then, the current will erode away the dirt beneath the root structure. Most of these generally have four to five feet of water in front of them, plenty of depth to hold a few good bass.

Emergent timber is a favorite spot to chase after bass. Knowing how to "see the forest for the trees" is most important in determining the bottom terrain and structure that may hold forage and bass.

Cypress Roots

Other root systems that are common in the southern U.S. are those of standing cypress trees. Sometimes called cypress 'knees', these roots often project up just above the surface of the water. Many are also hidden, depending on the water level, and they line the perimeter of the base of the tree. They can sometimes be a mess when completely intertwined.

These trees harbor lots of snakes and various amphibian forage. Fishing cypress roots with a sinking worm, however, can sometimes be difficult. Patience is the key to finding bass in these areas. The trees can be found in all depths of water, but the ones in the deeper water generally house the most bass. The isolated cypress trees in particular, also isolate the forage and can hold bass that are usually larger than the 'bank runner' in shallow water.

The backs of brushy coves with a fresh source of water, such as this one on Mexico's Lake Guerrero, are productive often and should be checked out. The break provided by the creek channel in the trees should be worked first, since most bass will be near the drop (into the creek bed) unless they have moved shallow in an explosive feeding mode.

Cypress trees are fairly fragile and are very susceptible to lightning and strong winds. Natural causes can pile up broken limbs and the upper torsos of weak trees on the lakebed near the trunk. Areas such as this, hold more than their share of forage and bass, and an angler only has to look up 'in the trees' for evidence of limbs missing.

On some southern lakes, partially standing cypress trees are the rule, rather than the exception. When water levels increase, the knuckle-eyes of the perimeter roots may not even pierce the surface, but the angler should be assured that they are present. The largemouth will be resting beneath the roots and submerged logs near the tree, awaiting an easy meal.

An angler should learn to look at the surface to determine whether or not there is a potential for submerged brush in the water. Once the angler can visualize what is beneath the surface, his chances are much better for success.

Flooded Jungles

Knowing the type of tree will often clue in an angler to the approximate depth of water in that area. For example, cypress and some hardwoods grow in low areas while pine tree stands grow on higher and initially dryer land. In a new reservoir with both tree types inundated, the shallower water will be covering pine, and cypress should be in the deeper water.

Heavy timber in a reservoir or natural body of water, not only provides fish with plenty of cover and food, but also camouflages the approach of the angler. Evidence of the boat or fisherman is filtered through the trees to the fish and it is often possible to work such heavy-duty structure very close without 'spooling' them.

A particulary effective way to fish the flooded jungles is with the injured-shad spoon. This method is very productive during late fall, winter, early spring, and even in midsummer. When the bass are deep in the woods, escaping from the very cold or very hot waters that are found shallower, vertical jigging with a spoon is hard to beat.

Creek bends and ledges within the flooded forests in 20 to 35 feet of water hold many bass which are prone to hit a well-presented lure. If you can't see the 'forest for the trees', then marker buoys can be used to pinpoint the submerged structure that you find either through visual interpretation or use of a depth locator. This is particularly important if all the trees look alike.

Most anglers know that submerged cedar trees generally provide better fishing than, say flooded pine trees. The pine will rot much quicker and have fewer small branches to provide cover for forage fish. But, have you ever analyzed a forest of flooded palm trees?

Some palm trees have smooth trunks while others have tough, rugged 'fronds' hanging on the trunks. For those unfamiliar with the term "frond", it is the remaining portion of a palm tree limb that is still attached to the trunk and

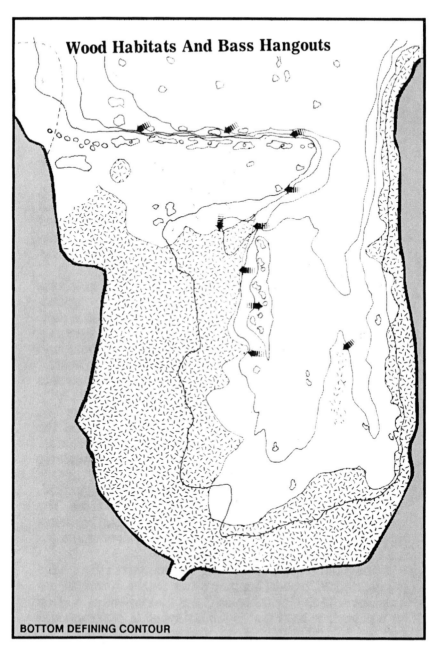

Wood Habitats And Bass Hangouts

BOTTOM DEFINING CONTOUR

normally broken off about one quarter of the way up the limb. The bark texture also varies from tree to tree. The more cover that a tree provides (via fronds or whatever), the more forage and other fish will be found.

Man-Made Wood

Pilings and docks provide excellent cover for food fish. Protection from predators is nearby in the form of a maze of posts. Fish can dart in and out of them to elude any predator. Baitfish are always in the vicinity. Crayfish frequent the rotting wood posts, and feed on microscopic organisms found beneath piers.

Shade, to protect the bass' lidless eyes, is abundant in these areas, and the water temperature can be slightly cooler. The endurance of a fish is greater in filtered light than in direct sun rays. Bass will usually be found shallower than you would normally expect in a lake, if they're using the piers and docks. Food, cover and protection are what bass demand and these are provided by docks and piers.

In many shallow, natural lakes and rivers, these man-made objects are 'dyn-o-mite'! They are a super attractor, often drawing a tremendous fish-per-acre population. Many of the flat, "dishpan" lakes have little natural structure (other than weed variations), and a pier or dock is an almost certain place to pick up some nice bass.

One of the first times that I concentrated soley on docks, piers, and pilings occurred several years ago. My cast landed three feet back under the pier and between two of

This figure shows a midwestern lake cove that is full of brush. Contact of largemouth, many in the five to seven pound range occurred where the four-feet depth contour coincided with brush. Other bass hideaways occurred at the quick drops in elevation. The shallow arm looked tremendous as a fishery, but the fish were only in a few areas.

the large support pilings. I lifted the rod tip immediately and the worm moved, but to the side, not toward me. I set the hook hard and was into a huge fish. The bass continued her run until the line touched the barnacle-clad piling and then, pop!

The fish had not wrapped the line around the dock post, but the line had been severed by merely touching the piling. It was a sad lesson to be learned. Fishing the docks did prove to be a worthwhile venture however, as my two companions and myself caught over 45 pounds or largemouth from the St. Johns River. Fishing with me that day were Ken Dykes of Orlando, and Steve Hamman, who lived in Jacksonville, Florida. Both men captured seven and one-half pound lunkers, as we probed the pilings and docks.

Where To Look

For many anglers, pilings and piers can prove to be a gold mine. Bass can usually be found using these structures, if the angler knows where to look. Certain docks, floating and post-supported, and pilings, are much better (naturally) than others, and attention to the differences will result in heavier stringers.

On some extremely flat, mud-bottomed lakes, a long pier may be used as a home. Bass will migrate along it and move into nearby weedbeds on feeding movements. For this reason, weedbeds in close proximity to docks and piers can be especially productive during feeding activity.

Steve Hamman and I were on a shallow central Florida lake one spring day when the bass started knocking shad out from under piers. I quickly switched from a plastic worm to a silver-finish Big "N", and took 3 bass on 3 casts. The shad and the bass then moved into the heavy grass beds which ran up to the pier area, and we followed. We methodically worked the area, and within a couple of hours had thirty-two pounds of largemouth in our live well. Then the activity concluded.

Bass are sneaky and sly. It's their nature, not any cunning, that determines this behavior. They'll move along

Docks and piers are numerous in many waters and in some, this may be the best structure near shore. Other cover may not be available and bass will find that which is, to live and search for forage. Dock bass are a special 'breed' of largemouth requiring special techniques for enticement. Proper lures, equipment, and a great deal of accuracy can justify a stringer full of fish.

breaks, keeping a low profile and remaining hidden as much as possible, until they see a victim to gobble up. They'll dart out from this protection, and grab their dinner upon locating it. What could be better protection for the bass than the support posts, when cruising toward shallow water?

Pier Pressure

Piers come in all shapes, sizes, lengths, and conditions. Some even have cabins on the end, several hundred feet from shore. Some are partially dilapidated, while others have brand new, unweathered pilings and cross-members. Most are wooden, but a few metal piers and posts can occasionally be found.

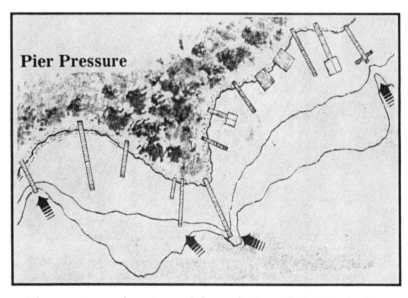

Pier Pressure

The two piers on the point, and the small pier at the left in the figure are potentially good. Possibly the pier shaped like a cross would be the next best bet to try. Although it does not reach into the deep water, there is a breakline projecting in at the point that the fish could use to get to. The 4 foot and 8 foot contours are shown, giving us a vivid example of productive and non-productive locations. Two of the piers shown have homes on the end of them, but the depth beneath the pier is only 2-3 feet. Two other piers are extremely wide, but again, the very shallow water prevents them from having very good bass fishing. The longest pier shown (toward the left in the figure) is on a flat, shallow piece of land and water. Very seldom will you find any large bass here.

A good pier to locate bass on will depend on several things. The most important characteristic is availability of forage. Close proximity to deep water is also important. Deep water is relative to the type of lake you're fishing. It could be 6 to 8 feet in some lakes, and 20 to 30 feet in others. If it doesn't meet this requirement, then your chances of finding bass under it are almost nil.

Another important thing to look for in selecting the pier to fish first, is the most shade. The piers with homes on the end of them are excellent. The wider piers which cast a wider shadow are prime territories. A long "skinny" pier, in shallow water, holds little forage and, in most cases, is a waste of time.

Another important consideration is the density and size of the support posts beneath the pier. The more dense (number of posts, cross-members near the water, etc.), the more productive a pier can be. The larger (in diameter) that these posts are, the better also. I've found, basically, that the more deep water and protection a pier offers the bass and their forage, the better the fishing will be.

How To Fish Piers And Pilings

The key to success, once you have selected the right structure to fish, is being thorough. You should start at one end and fish each support piling until you reach the other end. On an average sized pier, you should then move around the end and continue down the other side.

Do not think that one or two casts will find all fish under one pier. I've made several casts to the same piling and worked the area back and forth a few times before catching a nice bass.

Try to place your cast under the pier as far as possible. It takes a lot of practice to consistently place your cast exactly where you aim. I always try to get my lure 3 to 4 feet back up into the shade of the pier, if possible. This can sometimes be difficult, but it'll be very worthwhile. Until you can master the accuracy required, you'll get hang-ups and spend valuable time retrieving your lure from pilings or piers. But in pier fishing, casting accuracy is the name of the game.

Once you've worked the pier or row of pilings for their complete length, casting perpendicular to them, then move up next to them and work your lure parallel along them. Be a line watcher. Many times, as you retrieve your lure back through pilings, you'll notice it moving sideways before you can feel the strike, and the right time to set the hook when fishing pilings is two seconds ago!

Try to control the speed of your movement along the pier. If you move by quickly and only get in a few casts, then you'll be missing the fish. Don't believe that all the fish will be out on the end of the pier in the deepest water. Many times I've caught them in the middle of the pier's length.

BASS SERIES LIBRARY!

Six Great Books With A Wealth Of Information For Bass Fishermen

By Larry Larsen

I. FOLLOW THE FORAGE FOR BETTER BASS ANGLING - VOL. 1

BASS/PREY RELATIONSHIP - The most important key to catching bass is finding them in a feeding mood. Knowing the predominant forage, its activity and availability, as well as its location in a body of water will enable an angler to catch more and larger bass. Whether you fish artificial lures or live bait, you will benefit from this book.

SPECIAL FEATURES
- PREDATOR/FORAGE INTERACTION
- BASS FEEDING BEHAVIOR
- UNDERSTANDING BASS FORAGE
- BASS/PREY PREFERENCES
- FORAGE ACTIVITY CHART

II. FOLLOW THE FORAGE FOR BETTER BASS ANGLING -VOL. 2 TECHNIQUES - Beginners and veterans alike will achieve more success utilizing proven concepts that are based on predator/forage interactions. Understanding the reasons behind lure or bait success will result in highly productive, bass-catching patterns.

SPECIAL FEATURES
● LURE SELECTION CRITERIA
● EFFECTIVE PATTERN DEVELOPMENT
● NEW BASS CATCHING TACTICS
● FORAGING HABITAT
● BAIT AND LURE METHODS

III. BASS PRO STRATEGIES - Professional fishermen have opportunities to devote extended amounts of time to analyzing a body of water and planning a productive day on it. They know how changes in pH, water temperature, color and fluctuations affect bass fishing, and they know how to adapt to weather and topographical variations. This book reveals the methods that the country's most successful tournament anglers have employed to catch bass almost every time out. The reader's productivity should improve after spending a few hours with this compilation of techniques!

SPECIAL FEATURES
● MAPPING & WATER ELIMINATION
● LOCATE DEEP & SHALLOW BASS
● BOAT POSITION FACTORS
● WATER CHEMISTRY INFLUENCES
● TOPOGRAPHICAL TECHNIQUES

IV. BASS LURES - TRICKS & TECHNIQUES - Modifications of lures and development of new baits and techniques continue to keep the fare fresh, and that's important. Bass seem to become "accustomed" to the same artificials and presentations seen over and over again. As a result, they become harder to catch. It's the new approach that again sparks the interest of some largemouth. To that end, this book explores some of the latest ideas for modifying, rigging and using them. The lure modifications, tricks and techniques presented within these covers will work anywhere in the country.

SPECIAL FEATURES
● UNIQUE LURE MODIFICATIONS
● IN-DEPTH VARIABLE REASONING
● PRODUCTIVE PRESENTATIONS
● EFFECTIVE NEW RIGGINGS
● TECHNOLOGICAL ADVANCES

V. SHALLOW WATER BASS - Catching shallow water largemouth is not particularly difficult. Catching lots of them usually is. Even more challenging is catching lunker-size bass in seasons other than during the spring spawn. Anglers applying the information within the covers of this book on marshes, estuaries, reservoirs, lakes, creeks or small ponds should triple their results. The book details productive new tactics to apply to thin-water angling. Numerous photographs and figures easily define the optimal locations and proven methods to catch bass.

SPECIAL FEATURES
- UNDERSTANDING BASS/COVER INTERFACE
- METHODS TO LOCATE BASS CONCENTRATIONS
- ANALYSIS OF WATER TYPES
- TACTICS FOR SPECIFIC HABITATS
- LARSEN'S "FLORA FACTOR"

VI. BASS FISHING FACTS - This angler's guide to the lifestyles and behavior of the black bass is a reference source of sorts, never before compiled. The book explores the behavior of bass during pre- and post-spawn as well as during bedding season. It examines how bass utilize their senses to feed and how they respond to environmental factors. The book details how fishermen can be more productive by applying such knowledge to their bass angling. The information within the covers of this book includes those bass species, known as "other" bass, such as redeye, Suwannee, spotted, etc.

SPECIAL FEATURES
- BASS FORAGING MOTIVATORS
- DETAILED SPRING MOVEMENTS
- A LOOK AT BASS SENSES
- GENETIC INTRODUCTION/STUDIES
- MINOR BASS SPECIES & HABITATS

Breinigsville, PA USA
25 June 2010
240552BV00004B/3/P